FINANCIAL BASICS
FOR
SMALL BUSINESS SUCCESS

by James Gill

U.S. CHAMBER OF COMMERCE

SMALL BUSINESS INSTITUTE™

CREDITS

Editor: Beverly Manber

Layout/Design: ExecuStaff

Cover Design: Barry Littmann

Library of Congress 92-54356
ISBN-1-56052-167-8

ABOUT THE USCC SMALL BUSINESS INSTITUTE

The U.S. Chamber of Commerce Small Business Institute was formed to provide practical education and training resources for small business professionals and employees. The Institute offers practical and informative materials in:

- Marketing and Sales

- Budgeting and Finance

- Legal Issues

- Human Relations and Communication

- Productivity

- Quality and Customer Service

- Supervision, Management and Leadership

These ready reference materials, created for the U.S. Chamber by Crisp Publications, contain a wealth of useful advice for small businesses. The personal involvement exercises provide an opportunity to immediately apply what has been learned to your business.

While learning, it is easy to earn a Small Business Institute Certificate of Completion and valuable Continuing Education Units (CEUs). For more information or to enroll, call 800-884-2880.

THE U.S. CHAMBER OF COMMERCE
SMALL BUSINESS INSTITUTE

► **High Quality**
Up-to-date and to-the-point training and educational materials are selected by small business professionals.

► **Practical and Easy to Use**
You can immediately put to use the proven tips and techniques.

► **Cost-effective**
The courses come to you—you don't have to spend money on travelling to a training site or pay costly tuition.

► **Design Your Own Program**
Choose those courses that interest you most and meet the specific needs of your company.

► **Self-paced**
Learn when your schedule permits. Complete the coursework on your time.

► **Recognition and Reward**
Business owners and employees can earn Continuing Education Units (CEUs) as well as a Small Business Institute Certificate of Completion to recognize the achievement.

► **Quality Guaranteed**
All materials are unconditionally guaranteed. If you are not totally satisfied, simply return course materials within 30 days for a complete refund. No questions asked.

CONTENTS

CHAPTER ONE   DEVELOPING YOUR PLAN
                              AND STRATEGY   1
Setting Up Your System 3
Developing Financial Policies 4

CHAPTER TWO   THE BASICS   11
Learn the Terms..13
Glossary of Terms Used on the Balance Sheet 13
The Balance Sheet 14
Glossary of Terms Used on the Income Statement.................19
The Income Statement 19
Why Profit Doesn't Always Equal Cash 21
The Nature of Costs 21

CHAPTER THREE   PREPARE TO SUCCEED
                                IN YOUR BUSINESS   27
The Financial Plan 29
Developing the Pro-Forma Income Statement 29
Revised Cash Flow Chart...37

CHAPTER FOUR   PERCENTAGES AND RATIOS   41
Measure Your Progress 43
How Ratios are Developed 43
How to Use Ratios Without Fear 44
Introduction to Percentages 46
Hi-Tech Merchandise Company Percentages 50

CONTENTS (continued)

CHAPTER FIVE   **LIQUIDITY RATIOS**   **55**

Measuring Your Available Cash 57

Ratio: Current Ratio 61

Ratio: Cash Turnover 63

Ratio: Debt to Net Worth 64

Analysis 65

CHAPTER SIX   **PROFITABILITY RATIOS**   **69**

Measuring Your Profit, ROA, ROI and ROS 71

Ratio: Net Profit 74

Ratio: Rate of Return on Sales 75

Ratio: Rate of Return on Investment 76

Ratio: Rate of Return of Assets 78

Analysis of the Profitability Ratios 79

CHAPER SEVEN   **EFFICIENCY RATIOS**   **83**

Measuring How Well You Conduct Your Business.................85

Ratio: Average Collection Period for Accounts Receivable..........88

Ratio: Inventory Turnover 90

Ratio: Fixed Assets to Net Worth 92

Ratio: Investment Runover 93

CHAPTER EIGHT   **RATIO ANALYSIS**   **99**

Evaluate the Data 101

Data Collection Charts...101

What's Significant...110

CHAPTER NINE   **EXPENSE ANALYSIS**   **115**

Re-examine Your Expenses 117

The Cost of Goods Sold..118

What to Do When There Is No More Room to Cut...............119

Bartering 123

Joining an Exchange 123

CONTENTS (continued)

CHAPTER TEN   ASSET MANAGEMENT   127

Managing the Cash Account 129
Managing Receivables Policy 131
Inventory Management 133
Ordering Costs...135
Danger Signs 135
Reducing Obsolete Inventory..136
Leasing 137

**CHAPTER ELEVEN   HOW TO CONTROL
                          YOUR BUSINESS   141**

How to Forecast Finances 143
Trend Analysis 143
Pumping Iron Fitness Center Trend Analysis 148
Expenses Analysis 149
Analysis from the Balance Sheet 150
Hi-Tech Merchandise Company Trend Analysis 155
Limitations of Ratio Use 164
Controlling Credit 164
Accounts Receivable Aging Schedule 164
Credit Collection Tips 166
The Importance of Working Capital 168

CHAPTER TWELVE   FINANCIAL PLANNING   171

Managing Your Money 173
Breakeven Analysis 173
Cost Benefit Analysis..176

CONTENTS (continued)

CHAPTER THIRTEEN   EXPANDING YOUR BUSINESS   183

Learn to Plan Business Growth 185

Market Expansion 186

Obtaining Cost Information 187

Long-Term Arrangements 189

Neil Smith's 14 Rules for Expansion 192

CHAPTER FOURTEEN   SELLING YOUR BUSINESS   197

Prepare Yourself..199

Value Your Business 200

Prepare Your Business for Sale 202

APPENDIXES   207

ABOUT THE AUTHOR   235

CHAPTER ONE

DEVELOPING YOUR PLAN AND STRATEGY

SETTING UP YOUR SYSTEM

To help you get started in your new business, you will, of course, consult a good lawyer and banker. Don't forget that you should also select a qualified accountant, even if you or a family member intend to do your own bookkeeping. You will need to analyze the financial aspects of your business to get the best that it has to offer. An accountant can prepare this analysis, but you should interpret it and understand it well enough that you will have confidence to act on the information.

Your accounting records will be used throughout the life of your business. The users will range from you, the owner, to the Internal Revenue Service, government regulatory agencies, your investors or potential investors (if any), suppliers and lenders. If you seek credit from a supplier or wish to borrow to pay your bills, the bank or supplier will want to know that you can pay them. Therefore, setting up and maintaining your financial system are important. Selecting an accountant is the first step.

Public accountants or those that may be hired by the general public, may be self-employed or work for an accounting firm that serves the public. Most of these firms include at least one certified public accountant (CPA).

A CPA has met state education and experienced requirements and has passed a rigorous three-day exam.

Not all accountants have the same expertise. When you make your evaluations, consider if the candidate:

- ► Knows your industry
- ► Knows accounting procedures, how to summarize and present information that you understand
- ► Is aware of and will apprise you of possible legal pitfalls
- ► Will work with you on achieving your goals
- ► Will be available to you when needed
- ► Will ask questions that you should be asking

DEVELOPING FINANCIAL POLICIES

Before opening your doors for business, you should have five financial policies in place. They are systems and policies to handle 1) credit sales and 2) credit collection, 3) to determine depreciation and 4) inventory levels and 5) to set prices if needed.

1. Credit sales

If you plan to offer credit, you will need a credit policy. Criteria to consider are:

► Qualifications required to obtain credit

► How those qualifications will be checked and recorded

► How great a purchase should be required to qualify a customer for credit and at what amount credit should be stopped

► Type of billing cycle

► How slow payers will be handled

► How large a bad-debt account should be established

2. Credit collections

If you extend credit, chances are that you will have to spend some time collecting delinquent accounts. To do this and minimize your losses, be prepared before a system is needed.

► Maintain a receivables aging schedule

► Remind slow payers without upsetting them

► Know what you are willing to spend to collect what amount

► Check costs with credit collection agencies before you need them

► Act promptly on each delinquent account. Establish a time limit to send reminders, make phone calls, send harder-hitting follow-up letters and, finally, call a collection agency.

3. Depreciation

If you own any equipment or real estate with or without buildings, you need a depreciation policy to obtain the maximum tax break. Most small businesses determine depreciation by using one of the following methods.

► Straight line method

The simplest and most common depreciation calculation is the straight line method, which figures that the item depreciates the same amount each year. Divide the estimated useful life of an asset into its purchase price minus any salvage or resale value. This method is useful for accounting purposes, but it's not necessary for tax purposes.

► Accelerated methods

Many fixed assets are more valuable in their earlier years than in their later years, because, for example, equipment becomes more obsolete or inefficient as it ages. One accelerated depreciation method is called the double declining balance method. Another is the sum-of-the-years'-digits method. The effect of either method is to write off approximately two-thirds of the cost in the first half of the asset's estimated life.

Accelerated methods are used more for high tech items, such as computers. They simply speed up claiming depreciation. How this is done and which method to use is better explained by your accountant as every business is somewhat unique.

4. Inventory

Units of inventory are usually bought at varying times at different prices. Because of this, methods have been established to determine the cost of goods sold and the value of remaining inventory.

► Average cost method. Divide the total number of units of goods available for sale into the average purchase cost for a period of time. This cost should include freight and delivery charges to get the raw material to the manufacturer or the goods to the supplier. This number is the average cost of the inventory. The total number of goods sold during this period divided by the same average cost would equate to the cost of goods sold.

► FIFO (first in, first out). This method assumes that the inventory first acquired is the first used or sold, and the remaining inventory figure is the most recently purchased stock. Thus, the cost of goods sold reflects the earliest cost of purchases, and the remaining inventory figure reflects the most recent cost of the inventory. This method is balance sheet-based.

► LIFO (last in, first out). This method assumes that the inventory last acquired is the first used or sold and the remaining inventory figure is the oldest or first purchased. This method reflects the earliest cost of the inventory on the balance sheet and shows the most recent prices in the cost of good sold. Therefore, this method is income statement-based. Work with your accountant or tax preparer to help you find the best method of determining inventory for your particular type of business.

One method of setting the level of inventory to be carried is called the "economic order quantity."

Economic Order Quantity

How much and when to order may be issues you have to consider if you are in the resale or manufacturing business. Large orders usually mean lower cost per unit but larger inventories to keep. Smaller, more frequent orders lower the inventory figure but may not be economical if the unit cost is high.

A calculator with a square root key is very helpful for working the equation to determine an economic order quantity:

$$EOQ = \sqrt{\frac{2 \times S \times OP}{C \times P}}$$

EOQ = Economic order quantity

S   = Sales

OP = Cost to process each order

C   = Cost to carry the inventory, expressed as a percentage of the inventory value

P   = Price of each unit of inventory

If the company projects sales (S) of 10,000 units per year, which can be bought at (P) \$80 per unit, cost to carry the inventory (C) is 15% of the inventory's value, and it costs (OP) \$50 per order to process it.

$$\text{EOQ} = \sqrt{\frac{2 \times 10,000 \times \$50}{.15 \times \$80}} = \sqrt{\frac{20,000 \times \$50}{12}} =$$

$$\sqrt{\frac{1,000,000}{12}} = \sqrt{83,333.333} = 288.7 \text{ units} = \text{EOQ}$$

Therefore:

The average inventory is 288.7/2 144.3 or the halfway point

Average daily sales would be 10,000/360 = 27.8 units per day

A single order would last (**288.7** /27.8 Units per day = 10.4 days)

If it takes three days to deliver an order, then 3 x 27.8 = 83.4. This means that when 83.4 units are left, an order should be placed. Situations can vary. Since sales may be higher or lower and prices and delivery times may change, a safety stock is usually carried.

5. Setting prices

Price affects demand. The price you set will shape customer perceptions about quality, value and desire for your products or services. Price also helps determine your market share, competitive position and revenue. Some things you want to keep in mind when setting prices include:

▶ Don't look at margins as money in the bank and set prices accordingly. If the merchandise or service doesn't sell, the margin doesn't mean a thing.

▶ To maximize profits, the key is to set the price to cover cost and earn maximum revenue, yet obtain repeat business, referrals and customer loyalty. This sounds tough and it is, but it has been and is being done.

► If you want more market share and you set your price based on the industry average, you will probably do well during both the good and bad times, because stable prices prevent heavy discounting and allow you to match your competitors. This is especially important where products are similar and the goods or services are price-sensitive. Market share can be gained with other factors, such as product features, services, promotions and location.

► If you believe that you must have a certain return on you're investment from the product, then set a price objective accordingly. If you decide to use trade-ins, rebates, free service, free accessories, deferred billings, discounts for cash or early payment, quantity discounts for cash or early payment, quantity discounts, seasonal sales and loss-leader policies as incentives, you must set the price objective or margin to cover their cost.

► Competitors' prices and market forces, such as the economy and weather, can influence consumer buying decisions.

► Have a strategy in mind if your competitors cut prices, raise prices or do anything else that may affect you. Be sure to check how production, inventories, costs, cash flow and revenues will be affected by any change in price, because short-term success may spell long-term disaster if the money doesn't materialize.

ASK YOURSELF

▶ Outline criteria you will use in selecting an accountant.

▶ Develop written policies as appropriate for your business, for:

- Credit sales

- Credit collection

- Depreciation

- Inventory Economic Order Quantity

- Inventory valuation

▶ Establish a line of credit that your customers should not exceed.

▶ Develop your price policy.

▶ Evaluate your possible outside influences each year, quarter or month.

▶ Review your competitors' pricing policies.

▶ Describe how your pricing policy fits your image.

▶ Develop a plan to handle increased sales and your lower prices.

CHAPTER
TWO

THE

BASICS

LEARN THE TERMS

If you want to monitor the financial health of your business, you will need to keep a balance sheet and income statement. These documents are usually prepared by your accountant or a family member, and although it is not necessary that you become a bookkeeper or an accountant, you should understand how these statements are made and where the data comes from. More importantly, you should understand how to interpret these documents and use them to benefit your business.

Understanding and using financial statements is not difficult. Like almost everything, it takes a little learning and some practice. By going through this book a few times, especially by substituting your own statements for the practice problems, you will soon master financial analysis.

Some terms are used extensively on the balance sheet, and you should know what they are. The following glossary should help you understand what the balance sheet is and what it contains. Once this is mastered it will be only a short time until you can use this information to make your business a success.

GLOSSARY OF TERMS USED ON THE BALANCE SHEET

Assets. The money, merchandise, receipts, land, buildings and equipment that a company owns or that has monetary value.

Current assets. The sum of cash, notes, accounts receivable (minus reserves for bad debts), advances on inventories, inventories, and any other item that can be converted into cash in a short time, usually less than a year. Examples include cash, accounts receivable and inventory.

Fixed assets. Land, buildings, building equipment, fixtures, machinery, tools, furniture, office devices, patterns, drawings (minus salvage value and depreciation).

Liabilities. Everything that a company owes to a creditor; that is, the debts owed by the company to others. The two categories of liabilities are current liabilities and long-term debt.

Current liabilities. The total of all monies owed by the company that will fall due within one year. Examples include notes payable, accounts payable and accruals, which are taxes or wages that are accumulated against current profits but not yet due to be paid.

Long-term debt. All the obligations and any other monies that come due more than one year from the date of issuance. Sometimes called long-term liabilities.

Examples include a mortgage, legal paper that pledges property to cover a debt, and a term loan, a contract under which a company agrees to make interest and principal payments on specific dates to the lender over a period of time, usually three to 15 years.

Net worth. What the owner has represented on a balance sheet as the difference between all assets and all liabilities.

THE BALANCE SHEET

The typical balance sheet displays the assets of the business on the left side of the page and the liabilities and net worth on the right side of the page like this:

ASSETS = LIABILITIES

+

NET WORTH

The two types of assets are current assets and fixed assets. The two types of liabilities are current liabilities and long-term debt. The difference between all assets and all liabilities is net worth. That is, after you pay all your bills and notes, anything left is yours. It may not be cash, however. It could be things like accounts receivable, inventory or buildings and equipment. The formula is expressed as:

ASSETS − LIABILITIES = NET WORTH

or   ASSETS = LIABILITIES + NET WORTH

Why It's Called a Balance Sheet

The asset total on the left equals the total of the liabilities and net worth on the right. Because they are the same, they are said to be in balance. This is true even if the liabilities exceed the assets. (The net worth becomes negative, which means that it is subtracted from the liabilities instead of added.)

A balance sheet is designed to show how a business stands at *only* one point in time. It indicates how the money is distributed among generally recognized areas of the business such as cash, fixed assets, long-term debt, accounts payable, and so forth.

How a Balance Sheet is Prepared

A balance sheet uses the principle of double entry accounting (because each business action affects two or more accounts). A business action is a sale, purchase, borrowing, etc. An account can be cash, inventory and net worth. Accounts are placed in categories called current or fixed assets, current liabilities or long-term debt and net worth.

Let's suppose that a business was started, and the owner had $100,000. The owner borrowed $30,000, and $70,000 came from savings. The beginning balance sheet would look something like this:

CURRENT ASSETS		CURRENT LIABILITIES	
Cash	$100,000		0
		LONG-TERM DEBT	
		10 yr loan	$30,000
		NET WORTH	$70,000
	$100,000		$100,000

The owner decides to stock the store and purchases $50,000 of merchandise (inventory) but pays out only $25,000 in cash (cash reduced by $25,000 and a new account called inventory $50,000 added) and owes the other $25,000 (a new account called accounts payable, which is placed under the category of current liabilities). The revised balance sheet is shown on the following page.

CURRENT ASSETS		CURRENT LIABILITIES	
Cash	$75,000	Accounts payable	$25,000
Inventory	$50,000	LONG-TERM DEBT	$30,000
		NET WORTH	$70,000
TOTAL	$125,000	TOTAL	$125,000

The balance sheet is in balance with the addition of $25,000 that is owed to the vendor. It is placed under current liabilities because it is due to be paid back in less than a year.

Now let's suppose that the owner buys a building for $100,000, putting $25,000 down and obtaining a mortgage for $75,000 (another new account called mortgage $75,000, a reduction in cash by $25,000 and a new account under fixed assets, called building $100,000). The owner also buys some equipment costing $50,000 by putting $15,000 down and obtaining a 15-year note for $35,000 (a new account called 15 yr note $35,000, a reduction in cash for a total of $35,000 and a new account called equipment $50,000). The new balance sheet now appears as shown below:

CURRENT ASSETS		CURRENT LIABILITIES	
Cash	$35,000	Accounts payable	$25,000
Inventory	$50,000		
TOTAL CURRENT ASSETS	$85,000	TOTAL CURRENT LIABILITIES	$25,000
FIXED ASSETS		LONG-TERM DEBT	
Building	$100,000	10 yr note	$30,000
Equipment	$50,000	15 yr note	$35,000
		Mortgage	$75,000
TOTAL FIXED ASSETS	$150,000	TOTAL LONG-TERM DEBT	$140,000
		NET WORTH	$70,000
TOTAL	$235,000	TOTAL	$235,000

When sales are made, the inventory will reduce and the cash will increase, or if some sales are made on credit, a new account called accounts receivable will need to be added under current assets. Let's suppose that $25,000 of inventory is sold and that $15,000 is cash and $15,000 is on credit. ($5,000 is profit as inventory, which is usually shown at cost. In this case, profit appears as an increase in net worth, which presumes the amount of the sale was added to the balance sheet before any expenses were taken out.) The balance sheet now looks like this.

CURRENT ASSETS		CURRENT LIABILITIES	
Cash	$50,000	Accounts payable	$25,000
Accounts receivable	$15,000		
Inventory	$25,000		
TOTAL CURRENT ASSETS	$90,000	TOTAL CURRENT LIABILITIES	$25,000
FIXED ASSETS		LONG-TERM DEBT	
Building	$100,000	10 yr note	$30,000
Equipment	$50,000	15 yr note	$35,000
		Mortgage	$75,000
		TOTAL LONG-TERM DEBT	$140,000
TOTAL FIXED ASSETS	$150,000	NET WORTH	$75,000
TOTAL	$240,000	TOTAL	$240,000

The cycle begins again when the owner replaces the inventory.

Note that this business action affected three accounts on the asset side of the balance sheet: one account (inventory) lowered, the cash account increased and a new account called accounts receivable was added. One account on the right side, net worth, was affected. These business actions or transactions affected three accounts on the asset side of the balance sheet and only one account on the liability/net worth side, yet the statement is in balance.

To complete the balance sheet, the company name and address have been added, along with the date of preparation. The balance sheet shows how a business stands as of the date on the balance sheet.

GLOSSARY OF TERMS USED ON THE INCOME STATEMENT

You must also understand the income statement. The following glossary will clarify any unfamiliar terms. Once you comprehend these terms and how they are used, you can use the income statement to improve your business.

Net sales. The total dollar volume of all sales minus returns, allowances, discounts and rebates.

Cost of goods sold. For a retail or wholesale business, the price paid for merchandise plus the cost of having it delivered to the store during the accounting period. For a manufacturing firm, the cost of goods sold is the beginning inventory plus purchases, delivery costs, material, labor and overhead minus the ending inventory. A service business will probably not have a cost of goods sold account on its income statement because no "goods" are involved.

Gross profit. Sales less cost of goods leaves gross profit. It is the profit before expenses and federal taxes have been deducted.

Expenses. The cost of doing business. It includes such items as wages, telephone, insurance, depreciation, interest and advertising.

Net profit. The amount left over after deducting all due bills for the accounting period, plus interest and federal taxes. "Net profit" as used in this book will always mean profit before paying federal taxes.

THE INCOME STATEMENT

The income statement shows the total actions of a business over a period of time, be it a month or a year. It begins when sales are made, so the first entry, or account, would be sales. This is how the $30,000 in sales would look on the income statement.

Sales $30,000

The next entry is the cost of those goods sold, which was $25,000. The cost is subtracted from sales to show a gross profit of $5,000. The added entries would appear on the income statement as shown.

Sales	$30,000
Cost of Goods Sold	$25,000
Gross Profit	$5,000

The next entries are the expenses of running the business. (Note that the income statement has a heading and that it covers a period of time, in this case one month.)

INCOME STATEMENT

Fernelli Enterprises
Riverside, California
January 1 through January 31, 19xx

Sales		$30,000
Cost of Goods Sold		$25,000
Gross Profit		$5,000
EXPENSES		
Owner's drawings	$1,300	
Salaries	2,100	
Delivery	350	
Bad Debt	20	
Insurance	30	
Taxes (local)	10	
Interest	150	
Depreciation	100	
Advertising	180	
Total expenses		$4,240
NET PROFIT (before federal taxes)		$760

The total expenses are subtracted from the gross profit to give net profit before federal taxes of $760.

Your Turn

Develop a balance sheet and income statement using these figures.

Cash	$2,000	Mortgage	$25,000
Accruals	$6,000	Equip/fixtures	$50,000
Accts rec	$85,000	Inventory	$210,000
Land/bldg	$50,000	Net worth	$143,000
Accts pay	$205,000	Notes pay	$18,000
Drawings	$74,000	Delivery	$7,000
Sales	$700,000	Cost of goods sold	$500,000
Bad debt	$4,000	Wages	$65,000
Miscellaneous	$2,000	Advertising	$3,000
Interest	$8,700	Local taxes	$8,000
Insurance	$7,000	Depreciation	$4,000
Telephone	$2,000		

Answers are in Appendix D.

WHY PROFIT DOESN'T ALWAYS EQUAL CASH

Perhaps you have found out the hard way that showing a profit doesn't always mean you will have money in the bank. Uncollected credit sales will show up as an asset, which will translate into sales on the income statement. After the cost of goods sold and the other expenses are subtracted, a profit may be shown. It may be a large profit, but it still isn't cash!

Making a profit, at least on paper, does not necessarily mean you have a healthy business. Many firms have gone out of business while showing a profit. To stay in business and grow, a positive cash flow is required. If you can't pay your bills because you can't collect your debts, the best that can happen is that your suppliers and employees will simply quit you; the worst is an appearance in court.

THE NATURE OF COSTS

Every business is faced with costs. It is important to understand how they work as the business grows. The basic two types of costs—fixed and variable—are named because of their behavior. Fixed costs tend to remain the same for at least one year, while variable costs tend to change as the volume of business changes.

Stair-step or plateau behavior is another type of cost that is a mix of fixed and variable. This cost type is used mainly for utilities such as water, natural gas and sewage discharge and depends on the amount or volume that is used over a period of time. Usually the price goes down for each increment used. The cost is not dependent on time. It is a semifixed or semivariable cost and takes its name from the appearance of a stair step on a graph.

As a business owner you will be faced with some of each type of cost. Rent for your store or office space, insurance, taxes, subscriptions, and so on, are generally considered fixed costs. Hourly wages, advertising, telephone charges, utilities and consumables are generally considered to be variable costs.

The following chart illustrates fixed costs. The fixed cost line runs parallel to the horizontal line, and profit before taxes is measured on the vertical line after the sales line passes the fixed cost line. In the case below, the fixed costs are $1,000, the volume is 500 units sold, which makes the profit $1,000. The advantage of having all fixed costs is that once the costs are covered, all sales are profit. The disadvantage is that if the costs aren't covered, they must be paid anyway.

Example of All Fixed Costs & The Breakeven Point

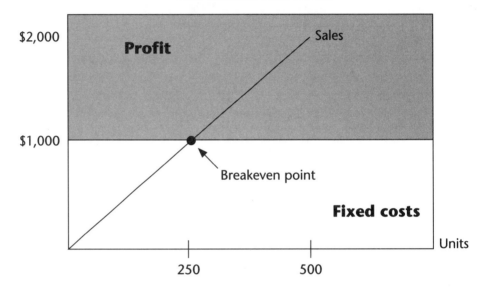

The following chart illustrates all variable costs; that is, those costs that accrue only when something is made or sold. The profit is measured the same way as with fixed costs. In this case the volume sold is 500 units, the variable cost is $1,000 and the profit or difference between what the cost was and the sales price of $2,000 is a profit of $1,000. The advantage is that you pay only for what you sell, assuming you have it on consignment, or what you make, assuming you only incur costs when you have a solid order. The disadvantage is that there is no leverage or any way to increase profits from operations. There is no Breakeven Point unless you wish to consider the Starting Point as the "Breakeven" Point.

Example of Variable Costs

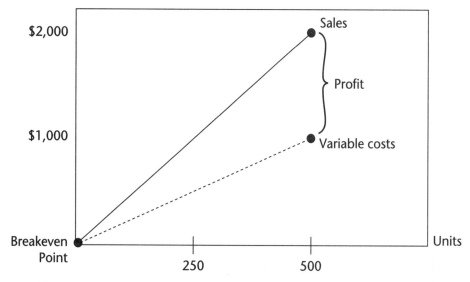

This chart combines both fixed and variable costs, which are found in most businesses whether retail, service or manufacturing. Profits accrue only when the sales line exceeds both fixed and variable cost lines. The point at which the sales line crosses the top cost line, usually the variable cost line, is called the breakeven point. This is the point at which the business just pays all its bills.

Example of Both Variable & Fixed Costs & The Breakeven Point

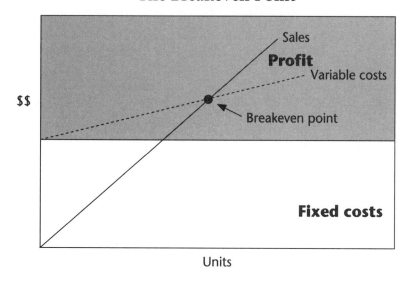

True or False

___ Variable costs increase as sales increase.

___ Fixed costs must be covered before you can realize a profit.

___ The balance sheet is a "snapshot" of the business because it reflects a certain condition at a certain time.

Answers are in Appendix D.

ASK YOURSELF

▶ What is the balance sheet equation?

▶ Describe the two types of assets and liabilities.

Assets:

Liabilities:

▶ Define the following:

Accounts receivable:

Long-term debt:

Net worth:

▶ Compare fixed and variable costs.

▶ Why does a balance sheet balance?

▶ Define the cost of goods sold for a retail store.

▶ Explain the difference between gross profit and net profit.

CHAPTER TWO

CHAPTER THREE

PREPARE TO SUCCEED IN YOUR BUSINESS

CHAPTER THREE

THE FINANCIAL PLAN

You are taking a huge risk when you start or expand a business, but you can minimize that risk if you plan. It makes no difference if you are starting from scratch, buying an existing business or expanding your business, you need to have a realistic plan based on careful research, investigation and analysis. Your data must include market research, a business and marketing plan and a financial plan.

The financial plan is based on market potential, your pricing strategy, sales forecast and knowledge of the facilities and equipment you will need to buy. This statement will help you predict your fixed and variable expenses for your type of business and aid you in obtaining start-up money.

If your data is accurate and objective, your financial plan will project your financial needs, breakeven point and profits for the next several months, first year and two additional years. This plan should be updated monthly and annually throughout your business life.

DEVELOPING THE PRO-FORMA INCOME STATEMENT

Pro-forma means a forecast, and, based on good data, the pro-forma income statement can serve not only as a guide but also help convince banks to loan you money or attract investors. This statement looks just like the income statement can serve not only as a guide but also help convince banks to loan you money or attract investors. This statement looks just like the income statement you use or will use in your business. It consists of:

Sales. Cash and credit sales—your total revenue from the business. Do not include any revenue not made from the business, such as interest from a savings account, certificate of deposit or other income. If you include other money, even interest on money already made by the business in past years, you won't have a true picture of the operating income, which will distort your decisions. If you are thinking of buying a business, watch out for this sort of distortion.

Cost of sales. Cost the merchandise if you retail it or sell by mail, etc. For manufacturing, see the glossary of terms, Chapter 2.

Gross margin or profit. The difference between sales dollars and cost of sales dollars. From this figure you will pay salaries, rent, advertising and other expenses.

Expenses. This includes such items as:

- ► Owner's drawings
- ► Salaries
- ► Vacation/sick days pay
- ► Health insurance
- ► Unemployment insurance
- ► Social security taxes
- ► Employee/owner life insurance
- ► Consumable supplies (used in the business; that is, not for sale)
- ► Repairs and maintenance (include decorations, painting, normal equipment repair and shop upkeep)
- ► Advertising
- ► Transportation (if used in the business; for example, delivery trucks, autos used by the business, and other necessary travel. Include tolls, parking, paid mileage or repairs to personal autos.)
- ► Professional expenses (may be itemized, for accounting, legal, consulting, etc.)
- ► Rent
- ► Telephone
- ► Utilities
- ► Fire, liability, property, product and worker's compensation insurance (this could be itemized depending on the business)

- ► Taxes, (excise, real estate, etc.)
- ► Interest
- ► Depreciation
- ► Leased equipment
- ► Miscellaneous (if this account is large, consider further expense breakdowns)
- ► Net profit (before federal taxes)

Anyone thinking of going into business should prepare pro-forma statements, both income and cash flow, before investing time, money and energy. To see how these documents work, let's develop a pro-forma income statement for the Pumping Iron Fitness Center.

Because this is a service business, there will be no cost of sales for the service, but there will be for the equipment that is purchased for resale. A fitness center requires cash up front to join, as do other service businesses.

The figures for sales, expenses and expected cash receipts that are used to prepare the pro-forma statements should be carefully researched. Talk to similar businesses, insurance agents, lawyers, accountants, the telephone company, leasing agencies, suppliers, bankers, federal agencies, radio and newspaper offices and anyone else who you can think of to achieve the best, most realistic data possible. Several data sources such as Robert Morris Associates, *The Small Business Reporter* or Dun and Bradstreet, (see Appendix A). Don't fool yourself with low guesses and incomplete information; and try to think about the economy, weather, and other possible influences in your trading area when making the sales forecast. You will need the best information you can get if you are borrowing money to begin your business.

Estimate each expense for 12 months, then estimate the next two yearly figures for a three-year budget and plan. Depending on the business, yours may take a year or more before it becomes fully self-sufficient.

Pumping Iron Fitness Center
Pro-Forma Income Statement
January 1, 19XX
( ) means negative figures

	1 Month	2 Month	3 Month	4 Month	5 Month	6 Month	7 Month	8 Month	9 Month	10 Month	11 Month	12 Month	2nd Year	3rd Year
Sales	$5,000	$5,400	$8,200	$9,200	$13,300	$12,500	$27,000	$28,000	$30,000	$33,000	$42,000	$40,000	$300,000	$325,000
Cost of Sales (equipment)	4,000	4,800	0	0	6,000	5,000	0	0	0	8,000	10,000	0	30,000	35,000
Gross Profit (service)	5,000	5,000	8,000	8,000	9,000	10,000	14,500	15,000	17,000	28,000	37,000	35,000	225,000	230,000
Gross Profit (equipment)	0	400	200	1,200	4,300	2,500	2,500	3,000	3,000	5,000	5,000	5,000	75,000	75,000
Total Gross Profit	1,000	600	8,200	9,200	7,300	7,500	27,000	28,000	30,000	25,000	32,000	40,000	270,000	290,000
Expenses:														
Owner's Drawings	470	470	1,270	1,270	1,270	1,270	1,270	1,270	1,270	1,770	1,570	1,370	40,000	40,100
Salaries	2,400	2,400	2,400	2,500	3,600	4,700	4,700	3,600	3,600	4,300	4,300	3,600	42,100	47,100
Vacation/Sick Days Pay	80	80	80	90	100	100	100	100	100	100	100	100	1,200	1,300
Health Insurance	130	130	130	150	195	195	195	195	195	195	195	195	2,140	2,340
Unemployment Insurance	40	40	40	60	60	60	60	80	80	80	80	80	960	1,000
Social Security/Workers Comp	100	100	100	105	115	120	130	130	130	130	130	130	1,400	1,450
Life Insurance	20	20	20	20	20	20	20	20	20	20	20	20	240	240
Consumable Supplies	100	100	100	100	100	100	100	100	100	100	100	100	1,200	1,200
Repairs and Maintenance	50	50	50	50	100	100	100	100	100	100	100	100	1,200	1,400
Advertising	400	400	400	400	400	400	400	400	400	400	400	400	4,800	5,000
Professional Expenses	150	150	150	150	150	150	150	150	150	150	150	150	1,800	1,800
Mortgage Principal	202	204	205	207	209	210	212	214	215	217	219	220	2,784	3,060
Loan Principal	903	910	918	926	934	941	949	957	965	973	981	989	12,496	13,914
Telephone	250	250	300	300	300	300	300	300	300	300	300	300	3,600	3,600
Utilities	300	300	300	300	300	300	300	300	300	300	300	300	3,600	3,600
Business Insurance	400	400	400	400	400	400	400	400	400	400	400	400	5,000	6,000
Taxes	380	380	380	380	380	380	380	380	380	380	380	380	4,560	4,560
Interest	2,175	2,166	2,157	2,148	2,138	2,128	2,120	2,110	2,100	2,090	2,081	2,070	24,041	22,447
Depreciation	1,830	1,830	1,830	1,830	1,830	1,830	1,830	1,830	1,830	1,830	1,830	1,830	21,960	21,960
Miscellaneous	100	100	100	100	100	100	100	100	100	100	100	100	1,500	2,500
Total Expenses	10,480	10,480	11,330	11,486	12,701	13,804	13,816	12,736	12,735	13,935	13,736	12,834	176,581	184,571
Net Profit	(9,480)	(9,880)	(3,130)	(2,286)	(5,401)	(6,304)	13,184	15,264	17,265	11,065	18,264	27,116	93,419	105,429

From this pro-forma income statement you can see that the business is not expected to break even until sometime in the fourth month. Note that the owners will need cash to pay bills until then. If some of these sales are credit sales, the money won't come in for 30–90 days, and some may not come in at all. Furthermore, the owners took a salary. This information is important for several reasons.

► It's a true business expense

► If the owners don't pay themselves, they won't know how the business is doing because they are subsidizing it

► If you expect to make a living from the business you must know what you can expect

► If you ever want to sell the business it will be overvalued unless you pay yourself

Another way to use this statement is to make two columns for each month and year, one for actuals and one for the budget or forecast. Another way to analyze your forecasts is to percentage the categories.

The Pro-Forma Cash Flow Chart

This chart calculates cash income and outgo. You must have cash to fuel your business, because you can't pay your bills from order forms.

To determine how much cash you will need and when you will need it, develop a cash flow chart. Use all the information on the pro-forma income statement except depreciation (depreciation is a noncash expense that may be deducted as an expense for tax purposes, but you don't have to pay it to anyone except yourself). To prepare the chart for a new venture, begin with a O column that will include all the investments you plan to make before you open your business. This column isn't necessary if you are buying a business: unless unusual arrangements are made, the cost of buying a business will show up in the form of a debt. So start with year one, month one.

Assume that you begin your business with $20,000 cash, which may come from borrowing, savings or selling your house. In the beginning column list all the pre-opening expenses. Starting with the first month of operations, list the sales, cost of any sales and all the expenses incurred.

Then subtract the column's expenses from the $20,000, and place the remainder ($600) as the starting cash figure in column 1. Next add it to the total cash-in figure ($5,000) and subtract the total cash-out figure ($12,650) to get the end-of-month (EOM) balance, a negative $7,050. This figure then becomes the starting cash figure for the next month.

To get the cash flow, subtract the cash-in figure only. Do not include accounts receivable or accounts payable. In this case, subtract $5,000 from the cash-out figure ($12,650). Note that both the EOM and the cash flow numbers may be negative, as shown.

Continue this method to the end of the statement to complete the cash flow chart.

This chart also indicates that the business won't generate enough cash from operations to support itself until the fourth month. However, it helps determine how much more money you should have as starting cash. This is done by adding the numbers in parentheses ( ), beginning with month one through month three for a total of $17,000. From this figure subtract the $600 left over from the original $20,000 for a new starting cash total of $36,400. This will provide a 0 cash balance in the third month.

Because we can't predict what will really happen, this is running a little too close. Therefore a contingency of extra cash should be available if you need it. Establish a line of credit with the bank so that you borrow only what you need and pay for only what you use, but more is there if necessary.

Pumping Iron Fitness Center
Pro-Forma Cash Flow Statement
January 1, 19XX
[- or ( ) means a negative figure]

	0 Month	1 Month	2 Month	3 Month	4 Month	5 Month	6 Month	7 Month	8 Month	9 Month	10 Month	11 Month	12 Month
Starting Cash	$20,000	600	(7,050)	(15,100)	(16,400)	(10,856)	(4,427)	2,199	$ 17,223	34,317	53,412	58,407	68,501
Cash-In:													
Cash Sales	0	5,000	5,000	8,000	11,000	17,000	12,000	18,000	20,000	27,000	20,000	27,000	35,000
Cash Rec'd	0	0	400	200	4,200	6,300	10,500	9,000	8,000	3,000	5,000	5,000	5,000
Total Cash-In	0	5,000	5,400	8,200	15,200	23,300	22,500	27,000	28,000	30,000	25,000	32,000	40,000
Cash-Out:													
Equipment	0	4,000	4,800	0	0	6,000	5,000	0	0	0	8,000	10,000	0
Owner's Drawings	0	470	470	1,270	1,270	1,270	1,270	1,270	1,270	1,270	1,770	1,570	1,370
Salaries	0	2,400	2,400	2,400	2,500	3,600	3,600	4,700	3,600	3,600	4,300	4,300	3,600
Vacation/Sick Days Pay	0	80	80	80	90	100	100	100	100	100	100	100	100
Health Insurance	0	130	130	130	150	195	195	195	195	195	195	195	195
Unemployment Insurance	0	40	40	40	60	60	60	60	80	80	80	80	80
Social Sec./Workers Comp	0	100	100	100	105	115	120	120	130	130	130	130	130
Life Insurance	0	20	20	20	20	20	20	20	20	20	20	20	20
Supplies	1,000	100	100	100	100	100	100	100	100	100	100	100	100
Repair/Maintenance	7,000	50	50	50	50	100	100	100	100	100	100	100	100
Advertising	4,400	400	400	400	400	400	400	400	400	400	400	400	400
Prof Expenses	2,000	150	150	150	150	150	150	150	150	150	150	150	150
Mortgage Principal	0	202	204	205	207	209	210	212	214	215	217	219	220
Loan Principal	0	903	910	918	926	934	941	949	957	965	973	981	989
Telephone	0	250	250	300	300	300	300	300	300	300	300	300	300
Utilities	0	300	300	300	300	300	300	300	300	300	300	300	300
Business Insurance	0	400	400	400	400	400	400	400	400	400	400	400	400
Taxes	0	380	380	380	380	380	380	380	380	380	330	380	380
Interest	0	2,175	2,166	2,157	2,148	2,138	2,128	2,120	2,110	2,100	2,090	2,081	2,070
Miscellaneous	5,000	100	100	100	100	100	100	100	100	100	100	100	100
Total Cash Out	19,400	12,650	13,450	9,500	9,656	16,871	15,874	11,976	10,906	10,905	20,005	21,906	11,004
EOM Balance	600	-7,050	-15,100	-16,400	-10,856	-4,427	2,199	17,223	34,317	53,412	58,407	68,501	97,497
Cash Flow	(19,400)	(7,650)	(8,050)	(1,300)	5,544	6,429	6,626	15,024	17,094	19,095	4,995	10,094	28,996

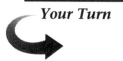

Your Turn   *Examine the cash flow statement below and answer the questions that follow.*

MONTHS

ITEMS	BEGIN	1ST	2ND	3RD	4TH	5TH
STARTING CASH	200	300	(200)	100	400	600
Cash-in						
Cash Sales	3,550	2,950	4,000	3,300	3,000	3,200
Cash Received	550	500	1,550	1,800	2,000	2,000
TOTAL CASH IN	4,100	3,450	5,550	5,100	5,000	5,200
CASH-OUT						
Purchases	1,000	1,000	2,500	2,000	2,000	2,000
Rent	600	600	600	600	600	600
Wages	2,050	2,050	2,050	2,050	2,050	2,050
Miscellaneous	350	300	100	150	150	150
TOTAL CASH-OUT:	4,000	3,950	5,250	4,800	4,800	4,800
Ending Balance		300	(200)	100	400	600	1,000
Cash Flow		100	(500)	300	300	200	400

This cash flow chart shows that there will be a $200 ending balance deficit at the end of the first month.

► Name three ways that the ending balance could at least equal zero.

► Will these same three ways also increase cash flow?

Answers are found in Appendix D.

REVISED CASH FLOW CHART

The revised cash flow statement shows the addition of $16,400. The cash flow between the two statements remains unchanged, because this figure is taken from cash received (cash-in) minus cash paid out (cash-out), and this portion of the statement did not change except for the last month, when the short-term loan was repaid. This loan could have been paid monthly or however you chose; any variation will have a direct influence on your cash flow. To make up or reduce the deficit of $16,400, you could not hire during the first few months, hold off on some expenses or sell memberships before opening. These "what if" techniques can be tried fairly easily and quickly with a computer and a spreadsheet to help you succeed before you even open your door.

Revised Income Statement

The next two pages show how selling more memberships would appear on the revised income statement. Note the insertion of a short-term loan to be repaid during the twelfth month.

Pro-Forma Balance Sheet

The next pro-forma statement is that of the balance sheet. The examples will show one prepared with the original income statement and the second prepared from the revised income statement at the end of year one.

Pumping Iron Fitness Center
Revised Pro-Forma Income Statement
January 1, 19XX

	1 Month	2 Month	3 Month	4 Month	5 Month	6 Month	7 Month	8 Month	9 Month	10 Month	11 Month	12 Month	2nd Year	3rd Year
Sales	$5,000	$5,400	$8,200	$15,200	$23,300	$22,500	$27,000	$28,000	$30,000	$33,000	$42,000	$40,000	$300,000	$325,000
Cost Of Sales (Equipment)	4,000	4,800	0	0	6,000	5,000	0	0	0	8,000	10,000	0	30,000	35,000
Gross Profit (Service)	5,000	5,000	8,000	14,000	29,000	20,000	24,500	20,000	27,000	28,000	37,000	35,000	225,000	230,000
Gross Profit (Equipment)	0	400	200	1,200	4,300	2,500	2,500	8,000	3,000	5,000	5,000	5,000	75,000	75,000
Total Gross Profit	1,000	600	8,200	15,200	17,300	17,500	27,000	28,000	30,000	25,000	32,000	40,000	270,000	290,000
Expenses:														
Owner's Drawings	470	470	1,270	1,270	1,270	1,270	1,270	1,270	1,270	1,770	1,570	1,370	40,000	40,100
Salaries	2,400	2,400	2,400	2,500	3,600	4,700	4,700	3,600	3,600	4,300	4,300	3,600	42,100	47,100
Vacation/Sick Leave	80	80	80	90	100	100	100	100	100	100	100	100	1,200	1,300
Health Insurance	130	130	130	150	195	195	195	195	195	195	195	195	2,140	2,340
Unemployment Insurance	40	40	40	60	60	60	60	80	80	80	80	80	960	1,000
Social Security/Workers Comp	100	100	100	105	115	120	130	130	130	130	130	130	1,400	1,450
Life Insurance	20	20	20	20	20	20	20	20	20	20	20	20	240	240
Consumable Supplies	100	100	100	100	100	100	100	100	100	100	100	100	1,200	1,200
Repairs and Maintenance	50	50	50	50	100	100	100	100	100	100	100	100	1,200	1,400
Advertising	400	400	400	400	400	400	400	400	400	400	400	400	4,800	5,000
Professional Expenses	150	150	150	150	150	150	150	150	150	150	150	150	1,800	1,800
Mortgage Principal	202	204	205	207	209	210	212	214	215	217	219	220	2,784	3,060
Loan Principal	903	910	918	926	934	941	949	957	965	973	981	989	12,496	13,914
Short-Term Loan												18,181		
Telephone	250	250	300	300	300	300	300	300	300	300	300	300	3,600	3,600
Utilities	300	300	300	300	300	300	300	300	300	300	300	300	3,600	3,600
Business Insurance	400	400	400	400	400	400	400	400	400	400	400	400	5,000	6,000
Taxes	380	380	380	380	380	380	380	380	380	380	380	380	4,560	4,560
Interest	2,175	2,166	2,157	2,148	2,138	2,128	2,120	2,110	2,100	2,090	2,081	2,070	24,041	22,447
Depreciation	1,830	1,830	1,830	1,830	1,830	1,830	1,830	1,830	1,830	1,830	1,830	1,830	21,960	21,960
Miscellaneous	100	100	100	100	100	100	100	100	100	100	100	100	1,500	2,500
Total Expenses	10,480	10,480	11,330	11,486	12,701	13,804	13,816	12,736	12,735	13,935	13,736	31,015	176,581	184,571
Net Profit	(9,480)	(9,880)	(3,130)	3,714	4,599	3,696	13,184	15,264	17,265	11,065	18,264	8,985	93,419	105,429

Beginning balance sheet:

Pumping Iron Fitness Center
Pro-Forma Balance Sheet
January 1, 19XX

Assets		Liabilities	
Current Assets		Current Liabilities	0
Cash	600	Long-Term Debt	
Accounts Receivable	0	10 Year Note	185,000
Inventory	0	Mortgage	80,000
Supplies	6,000		
Fixed Assets		Net Worth	11,600
Building	110,000		
Equipment/Fixtures	160,000		
Total	$276,600		$276,600

Pumping Iron Fitness Center
Pro-Forma Balance Sheet
January 1, 19XX

Assets		Liabilities	
Current Assets		Current Liabilities	
Cash	$30,000	Accounts Payable	$20,000
Accounts Receivable	5,000	Accruals	16,000
Inventory	14,200		
Fixed Assets		Long-Term Debt	
Building	106,400	10 Year Note	173,654
Equipment/Fixtures	158,500	Mortgage	77,466
		Net Worth	26,980
Total	$314,100		$314,100

ASK YOURSELF

► Why is it important to be realistic when you develop your pro-forma income statement?

► What can you learn from a cash flow chart?

► List good sources of information for your pro-forma statements.

► Discuss the various sources of available money.

CHAPTER
FOUR

PERCENTAGES
AND
RATIOS

Ratios are used every day. Sometimes they illuminate relationships better than anything else. For instance, miles per gallon or the unemployment rate are ratios that are easier to grasp than the total number of unemployed people or the total number of gallons of gas used. We look for the best price per ounce for food, we compare batting averages of baseball players and we measure the cost of building by dollars per square foot. Ratios are also an important tool to measure your business progress and to compare your business to your competitors or your industry.

HOW RATIOS ARE DEVELOPED

Ratios are expressed by placing one number over another number. The number on top represents the figure you want to compare, and you are comparing it to the bottom figure, or base. For example, 50/100 is a ratio. It means that 50 is to be divided by 100. The answer is .50 or 50%. That is, if you have $50 in sales and $100 of fixed assets such as a piece of equipment or a fixture, the sales amount to one half the value of the fixed assets, or a return on fixed assets of 50%.

Your Turn   ***Calculate the following ratios.***

$$\frac{\$41{,}000}{33{,}000} = \qquad\qquad \frac{\$60{,}000}{6{,}000} =$$

$$\frac{\$15{,}000}{23{,}500} = \qquad\qquad \frac{\$48{,}000}{23{,}000} =$$

$$\frac{\$9{,}125{,}000}{60{,}000} = \qquad\qquad \frac{\$25{,}000}{23{,}500} =$$

$$\frac{\$2{,}000}{23{,}500} = \qquad\qquad \frac{\$60{,}000}{71{,}000} =$$

Answers are found in Appendix D.

Ratios are used as indicators of how your business is doing. They do not make decisions for you but will provide information from which decisions may be made.

Ratios measure proportions and relationships by having you translate your assets (such as tools and inventory) and liabilities (such as payables and loans) into dollar figures. By doing this it is easy to see the relationship of two seemingly unrelated items. Ratios also let you compare two time periods. For example, you can use a ratio to measure your inventory turnover from month to month or year to year.

Let's keep things in the proper perspective. Suppose you are asked to take a chance (and you only get one chance) that would pay you $100,000. All you have to do is call "heads" or "tails" at the flip of a coin. You have a 50-50 chance of winning, but you have to risk 10% of that amount, or $10,000. You might shy away from having to put up so much money, even though the payoff was quite large. However, you might be willing to risk $10% of $100, or $10, to win the $100. Even though the percentage is the same, the amount of real money makes a difference. Therefore ratios and percentages need to be kept in context, because they represent real dollars to your business.

HOW TO USE RATIOS WITHOUT FEAR

Think of ratios as one of your best friends when scrutinizing your business. They are simple to calculate, easy to use and provide a wealth of information that cannot be gotten anywhere else.

Ratios are aids to judgment and cannot take the place of experience. They will not replace good management, but they will make a good manager better. They help to pinpoint areas that need investigation and assist in developing an operating strategy for the future.

To ease you into the use of ratios, review the five basic rules.

1. To determine a percentage change, let's suppose your sales increased 25% the first month of the year and 37% the second month. The last increase was not a 12% increase, because both increases are taken from the same base pe-

riod, which in this case is 100. To determine the increase, divide the 12 points by the new base period, which is 125 (the beginning figure plus the first month's figure) for a true increase of 9.5%.

2. When comparing a part to a whole, such as net profits to sales, the whole is always the base because net profits are a part of the sales dollar. Without sales there would be no net profit; therefore, net profits is the part and sales the whole.

3. A percent of something can increase by more than 100% but cannot decrease by more than 100%. Think of it like this: You can double (200%) your money many times, but you can lose all of it (100%) only once.

4. Ratios lose significance and accuracy when they become excessively detailed. This is important, because it means that you don't need all the data or figures to use ratio analysis and this form of analysis should be used for estimates.

5. Ratios are to assist you in decision making, not make the decisions for you.

Ratios can help you make decisions, but they should be used with caution. Always remember:

► Maintain an objective attitude. Don't use ratios to support your predetermined conclusions. Use them to help you understand your business.

► Don't use the wrong figures. For instance, when looking at a percent change between two dollar figures (such as a raise in price from $2 to $3), the number you want to compare is the difference between the two dollar price figures, which is $1. This figure is then divided by $2 for a percent raise of 50%. The "whole" is the original price. If the price dropped a dollar from $3 to $2, then divide the $1 drop by the original price—$3.

► Don't compare numbers that don't have meaning: for example, expenses to fixed assets. This number is easy to calculate but has no meaning in the operation of a business.

INTRODUCTION TO PERCENTAGES

Percentages are useful to compare and analyze business operations and transactions. For accuracy you need to compare your company to one like yours or a standard compiled of the same size companies within the same industry.

The first part of the analysis will be to look at the percentages of each account and expense and compare them to a standard or average for the industry. The percentages and ratios are taken from leading companies, those in the upper quartile, which will be used as a standard. A standard may also be a goal you set for yourself, something to measure your progress and a way to see what you might have to change in your percentages or ratios—hence the accounts themselves—to expand, add a new product or go for a larger market share.

The balance sheets and income statements for the Pumping Iron Fitness Center, a service company, and the Hi-Tech Merchandise Company, a retailer/assembler, will be analyzed in terms of percentages and ratios. Let's first look at the Pumping Iron Fitness Center and compare accounts and expenses to the standard, then look at the ratios that indicate relationships between accounts.

Pumping Iron Fitness Center

Balance Sheet

January 1, 19XX

Assets			Ind	Liabilities				Ind
		%	Std%				%	Std%
Current Assets				Current Liabilities				
Cash	$30,000	9.5	8.9*	Accounts Payable	$20,000		6.4	5.2*
Accounts Receivable	5,000	1.6	15.3*	Accruals	16,000		5.0	5.0*
Inventory	14,200	4.5	4.2*					
Fixed Assets				Long-Term Debt				
Building	106,400	33.9	68.8	10 Year Note	173,654	55.3		26.8*
Equipment/Fix	158,500	50.5		Mortgage	77,466	24.7		
				Net Worth	26,980		8.6	37.6
Total	$314,100	100	97.2*		$314,100	100		74.6*

*2.8% other assets

*21.1 other current liabilities
*4.3 other long-term debt

Pumping Iron Fitness Center
Income Statement
January 1, 19XX

			%	Ind Std%
SALES	$300,000		100	100
(Credit Sales $42,600)			14.2	
Cost of Sales (equipment)	30,000		10.0	11.5
Gross Profit (service)		225,000	75.0	
Gross Profit (equipment)	———	75,000	25.0	
Total Gross Profit	270,000		90.0	88.5
EXPENSES				
Owner's Drawings	40,000		13.3	N/A
Salaries	42,100		14.0	23.5
Vacation/Sick Days Pay	1,130		.4	
Health Insurance	3,900		1.3	
Unemployment Insurance	760		.3	6.6
Social Security Taxes	700		.2	
Life Insurance	1,800		.6	
Consumable Supplies	1,200		.4	1.0
Repairs and Maintenance	1,000		.4	2.7
Advertising	4,800		1.6	1.6
Professional Expenses	1,800		.6	0
Mortgage Principal	2,534		.8	0
Loan Principal	11,346		3.8	0
Telephone	3,500		1.2	3.8
Utilities	3,600		1.2	6.6
Insurance	3,000		1.0	1.6
Taxes	4,560		1.5	2.5
Interest	25,483		8.5	4.5
Depreciation	21,960		7.3	5.5
Miscellaneous	1,200		.4	0
Total Expenses	$176,373		58.8	59.9
Net Profit		$93,627	31.2	28.6

N/A=Not available.   ( )=Indicates additional information

From the balance sheet, note that the Fitness Center has good cash availability but is weaker in accounts receivable and inventory. This start-up should strive to keep the strong cash and inventory position and possibly can seek more sales by extending credit and still stay in business. Credit sales are a local issue, and the owner must decide if they will be collectable and increase business.

Fixed assets are about 20% above the average, but this is a start-up with new equipment; fixed assets will drop as business increases and more money flows into current assets. Current liabilities appear to be standard, but long-term debt is not. Long-term debt will improve as debts are reduced, which will also help net worth—which is clearly very low at this time.

Not all—but enough—industry standard percentages were available to reflect the expenses on this income statement. Cost of sales and gross profit are average. In our example, 1% is more than $3,000. If money is tight in your business, translate the percentages into real money and see if you would reach the same decisions.

Salaries appear to be a little low at the Pumping Iron Fitness Center unless we add in the owner's salary. The benefits also seem to be low, which is to be expected with low salaries. Repairs and maintenance are low, which may be because it is an almost new facility and the equipment doesn't need much repair. Interest and depreciation figures are higher, but since we are not comparing one start-up to another, some leeway is acceptable. Total expenses are better than the average. Interest and depreciation are higher, which can be expected. The troubling area seems to be the drawings, salaries and benefits. If this company is making money, I would conclude that the industry averages included both the salaries and benefits in the same category. If not, this may be a concern. As other expenses increase over time, profit percent will decline. Net profit is in good shape, partly because cost of goods sold is low and partly because expenses are low.

These are the sort of things to look for when doing an analysis.

Your Turn   *Determine the percentages of each account in the balance sheet and income statement below.*

Consulting R We
Balance Sheet
2nd Year 19XX

ASSETS	DOLLARS	%	LIABILITIES	DOLLARS	%
Cash	15,000		Notes Payable	8,000	
Receivables	10,000		Trade Payable	6,500	
Inventory	2,000		Accruals	10,000	
Investments	11,500		LTD Due	500	
Current Assets	38,500		Current Liability	25,000	
Fixed Assets	21,000		Long-Term Debt	14,500	
			Net Worth	20,000	____
Total Assets	59,500	100	Total Liability	59,500	100

Income Statement

SALES/RECEIPTS	$75,000	%/100

EXPENSES		
Drawings	$30,000	
Wages	8,000	
Advertising	3,000	
Legal/Accounting	1,500	
Maintenance	800	
Supplies	250	
Telephone	1,800	
Miscellaneous	150	
Depreciation	$3,000	
Interest	1,000	
Rent	10,000	
Utilities	2,000	
Insurance	750	
Taxes/License	850	

TOTAL EXPENSES	$63,100	%

NET PROFIT $11,900

% = Percentage for Consulting R We   %IA = Percent of the industry average

Answers are found in Appendix D.

HI-TECH MERCHANDISE COMPANY PERCENTAGES

Now let's examine the Hi-Tech Merchandise Company's balance sheet and income statement.

HI-Tech Merchandise Company
Balance Sheet
January 1, 19XX

Assets				Liabilities			
			Ind				Ind
Current Assets		%	Std%	Current Liabilities		%	Std%
Cash	$52,000	7.8	8.1*	Notes Payable	$58,000	8.8	19.1
Accounts Receivable	185,000	28.0	31.2*	Accounts Payable	205,000	31.0	20.4
Inventory	200,000	30.3	34.3*	Accruals	46,000	6.9	16.3
Fixed Assets				Long-Term Debt			
Land/Building	150,000	26.6	24.4	Mortgage	104,300	15.8	18.7
Equipment/Fix	75,000	11.3		8 Year Note	63,000	9.5	
				Net Worth	185,700	28.0	25.5
TOTAL	$662,000	104	98.0*	TOTAL	$662,000	100	100

2% other current assets

Hi-Tech Merchandise Company
Income Statement
January 1, 19XX

		%	Ind Std%
Net Sales (minus Allow and Discounts)	$766,990	100	100
(Credit Sales 575,000)		75	
Cost of Goods Sold	560,000	73	63.7
Gross Profits	206,990	27	36.3
Expenses			
Drawings	$14,000	1.8	1.3
Wages	65,000	8.5	13.4
Benefits/Social Security	7,790	1.0	2.6
Delivery	12,200	1.6	3.7
Bad Debt	4,000	.5	.2

(continues on next page)

(continued)

Professional	2,000	.3	.7
Telephone	2,000	.3	.6
Depreciation	24,000	3.2	5.2
Repairs/Consumable Supplies	2,200	.3	.8
Life Insurance	1,800	.2	
Utilities	3,000	.4	.7
Insurance	7,000	.9	.8
Taxes	8,000	1.0	3.2
Interest	12,447	1.6	1.4
Loan principal	7,875	1.0	
Mortgage principal	2,477	.4	
Advertising	5,000	.6	1.1
Miscellaneous	7,000	.9	
Total Expenses	187,789	24.5	35.7
Net Profit	$19,201	2.5	4.2

Not all percentages were available, but enough were available to compare our example to the industry average.

This start-up's current assets are about 8% lower than the average. More credit sales could be made if this is holding back sales, and the inventory could be increased slightly if this is a factor in making sales. To increase inventory takes cash, and the cash account is a little low; however, faster collection of accounts receivable could help these problems.

Fixed assets are about 10% higher than average, possibly owing to the start use of newer equipment and fixtures.

Current liabilities show that notes payable and accruals are less than standard, but accounts payable are greater. The accounts payable probably has a relationship to the inventory that hasn't been sold. As more cash is received, either by speeding up collections or increasing cash sales, the large accounts payable account will decrease.

Long-term debt is within 10% of the standard, and as it is paid, it will reach the standard. Net worth is about right. This business appears to be on the right track and only needs to watch sales and cash flow.

The income statement indicates that the cost of goods sold is almost 10% more than the standard. Perhaps the stock could be purchased more inexpensively elsewhere, or perhaps the company had to pay a premium or late payment because of a lack of ready cash. It could be that the standard includes some discount for volume or early payment. Salaries appear to be lower, but this may not be a direct comparison. The interest expense is close to the standard. Depreciation, however, is a little lower than the standard and may be due to owning an older building. Taxes may include license fees, and an extra local tax may be reflected in the average.

REVIEW

Ratios help us understand the relationship between two things and are expressed as either a percent or a proportion. Ratios are developed by dividing the number you wish to compare by the base number. Batting averages, miles per gallon and price per ounce are ratios that we use every day.

Ratios are expressed as: $\dfrac{50}{100}$ = 50% or 1 to 2 (1:2)

$\dfrac{100}{50}$ = 2 times or 2 to 1 (2:1)

If the top number is smaller than the bottom number, the ratio will be a percent. If the top number is larger than the bottom number, the ratio will be expressed as "times."

Percents provide us with a tool to do common-size analysis, which is particularly helpful in comparing the dollar figures on the balance sheet and income statement.

By doing this comparison to other companies, an industry standard or your own company's percentages over time, trends can be noted and targets defined.

Percents provide an excellent means to make comparisons and note relationships without worrying about the dollar amounts. Percentages are better target figures than dollar amounts because they allow equal comparisons between a large company and a small company.

ASK YOURSELF

▶ Why we do ratio analysis?

▶ How are ratios developed and used?

▶ What do ratios measure?

▶ Describe the five basic rules of ratios.

▶ How would you develop common-size balance sheets and income statements?

CHAPTER FOUR

CHAPTER
FIVE

LIQUIDITY

RATIOS

MEASURING YOUR AVAILABLE CASH

Several common ratios are used to measure and control a business: liquidity, profitability and efficiency. A fourth set is also used if you sell common stock to finance your business (see Appendix B). However, most small business owners don't usually sell common stock to raise capital, and you will not use every ratio, especially if you are in a service business such as the Pumping Iron Fitness Center.

The first set of ratios, liquidity ratios, measure the amount of cash available to cover both current and long-term expenses. These ratios are especially important in keeping your business alive, because running short of cash and not being able to pay your bills is the fastest way to go out of business. Furthermore, lending institutions don't necessarily want to loan money when you need it. Make arrangements for a line of credit when your business liquidity looks very good and get it in writing.

Profitability ratios measure and help you control your income through higher sales, larger margins, getting more from your expenses or a combination of these methods.

Efficiency ratios measure and help you conduct your business. They add another dimension to increasing your income by assessing such important transactions as your use of credit, inventory and assets.

Liquidity, profitability and efficiency ratios will be developed and analyzed from the balance sheets and income statements of the Pumping Iron Fitness Center and the Hi-Tech Merchandise Company. The efficiency ratios will pertain to almost any new business, whether it was started from scratch or bought as an existing business.

A more proper way to obtain "average inventory," which indicates a beginning and an ending inventory figure, will be shown in Chapter 11, How to Control Your Business. The figure on the balance sheet will be used as the average inventory figure to discuss the types of ratios.

Pumping Iron Fitness Center

Balance Sheet

January 1, 19XX

Assets			Liabilities		
Current Assets			**Current Liabilities**		
Cash	$30,000		Accounts Payable	$20,000	
Accounts Receivable	5,000		Accruals	16,000	
Inventory	14,200				
Fixed Assets			**Long-Term Debt**		
Building	106,400		10 Year Note	173,654	
Equipment/Fixtures	158,500		Mortgage	77,466	
			Net Worth	26,980	
Total	$314,100			$314,100	

Pumping Iron Fitness Center

Income Statement

January 1, 19XX

Sales	$300,000	
(Credit Sales $42,600)		
Cost of Sales (equipment)	30,000	
Gross Profit (service)		225,000
Gross Profit (equipment)		75,000
Total Gross Profit	270,000	
Expenses		
Owner's Drawings	40,000	
Salaries	42,100	
Vacation/Sick Days Pay	1,130	
Health Insurance	3,900	
Unemployment Insurance	760	
Social Security Taxes	700	
Life Insurance	1,800	
Consumable Supplies	1,200	
Repairs and Maintenance	1,000	
Advertising	4,800	

(continues on next page)

(continued)

Professional Expenses	1,800
Mortgage Principal	2,534
Loan Principal	11,346
Telephone	3,500
Utilities	3,600
Insurance	3,000
Taxes	4,560
Interest	25,483
Depreciation	21,960
Miscellaneous	1,200

Total Expenses $176,373

Net Profit $93,627

Hi-Tech Merchandise Company
Balance Sheet
January 1, 19XX

Assets		Liabilities	
Current Assets		**Current Liabilities**	
Cash	$52,000	Notes Payable	$58,000
Accounts Receivable	185,000	Accounts Payable	205,000
Inventory	200,000	Accruals	46,000
Fixed Assets		**Long-Term Debt**	
Land/Building	150,000	Mortgage	104,300
Equipment/Fixtures	75,000	8 Year Note	63,000
		Net Worth	185,700
TOTAL	$662,000	TOTAL	$662,000

Hi-Tech Merchandise Company
Income Statement
January 1, 19XX

Net Sales (minus allowances and discounts)		$766,990
(Credit sales $575,300)		
Cost of Goods Sold		560,000
Gross Profit		206,990

Expenses

Owner's Drawings	$14,000	
Wages	65,000	
Benefits/Social Security	7,790	
Delivery	12,200	
Bad Debt	4,000	
Professional	2,000	
Telephone	2,000	
Depreciation	24,000	
Repairs/Consumable Supplies	2,200	
Life Insurance	1,800	
Utilities	3,000	
Insurance	7,000	
Taxes	8,000	
Interest	12,447	
Loan Principal	7,875	
Mortgage Principal	2,477	
Advertising	5,000	
Miscellaneous	7,000	
Total Expenses	187,789	
Net Profit		$19,201

Liquidity ratios help in determining your firm's ability to pay its bills on time. Depending on your type of business, the amount of ready cash will vary owing to the season, the timing of a sale or the health of the national or international economy.

However, no business should let its cash reserves drop below a certain limit. By knowing these limits you can regulate your planned spending or borrowing to help your business grow at the rate you can support. The health of your business is like your personal health—a balance is necessary. While you require the right type of food and a certain amount of sleep, your business requires that you don't overspend or oversave if your cash is to work properly for you.

RATIO: CURRENT RATIO

Generally accepted standards and industrial averages may not fit your business even though it may resemble one of the examples. Consult your trade association, small business office or one of the references listed in Appendix A for more information.

Pumping Iron Fitness Center (service)

$$\frac{\text{Current Assets}}{\text{Current Liabilities}} \quad \frac{49,200}{36,000} = 1.4 \text{ times}$$

Hi-Tech Merchandise Company (Retail/assembly)

$$\frac{\text{Current Assets}}{\text{Current Liabilities}} \quad \frac{437,000}{309,000} = 1.4 \text{ times}$$

Measures: The ability to meet short-term obligations

Generally accepted standard: 2:1 for both companies

Low ratio means: A company may not be able to pay off its bills as rapidly as it should, take advantage of cash discounts or other favorable terms or keep its suppliers happy and receive eager service.

High ratio means: Money that could be working for the business is tied up in government securities, cash savings or other safe funds.

Remarks: The proper ratio depends on the kind of business, the time in the business cycle and the age of the business.

Another variation is the acid test or quick ratio, which is the same as the current ratio except it eliminates inventory so that only cash and accounts receivable are counted. Some analysts reduce accounts receivable by 25% before using this ratio. Whether you do or not depends on how much faith you have in your ability to collect your debts. The ratio looks like this:

Pumping Iron Fitness Center

$$\frac{\text{Cash + Accounts Receivable}}{\text{Current Liabilities}} = \frac{35,000}{36,000} = 97\%$$

Hi-Tech Merchandise Company

$$\frac{\text{Cash + Accounts Receivable}}{\text{Current Liabilities}} = \frac{237,000}{309,000} = 77\%$$

A safe margin would be at least 1:1. The service business comes close to having a safe margin and the retail business is slightly over three-quarters to meeting a 1:1 safe margin.

Your Turn

Answer these following:

▶ *Are these ratios high or low compared to the standard?*

The Standard is 2.2 times   High   Low   High   Low

$$\frac{\text{Current Assets}}{\text{Current Liabilities}} =$$
    1.7 ☐   ☐   2.6 ☐   ☐

▶ Which would you want in your business?

▶ Why?

Answers are found in Appendix D.

RATIO: CASH TURNOVER

Pumping Iron Fitness Center

$$\frac{\text{Sales}}{\text{Working Capital}} \quad \frac{300,000}{13,200} = 22.7 \text{ times}$$

Hi-Tech Merchandise Company

$$\frac{\text{Sales}}{\text{Working Capital}} \quad \frac{766,990}{128,000} = 6.0 \text{ times}$$

(Working capital = current assets – current liabilities)

Pumping Iron Fitness Center

$49,200 – $36,000 = $13,200

Hi-Tech Merchandise Company

$437,000 – $309,000 = $128,000

Working capital is the money you must have to operate your business on a daily basis—to pay salaries and other bills. The amount of working capital changes every time you receive cash, make a sale, write a check or make a payment.

Measures: The turnover of cash or working capital. Maintaining a positive cash flow or working capital balance will provide an adequate means to finance your sales without struggling to pay for the material or goods you are buying.

Generally accepted standards: Five or six times for both companies unless there is a seasonal high or low time, in which case the standard will rise or fall to support sales.

Low ratio means: You may have the funds tied up in short-term, low-yielding assets. This means that you may get by on less cash.

High ratio means: A vulnerability to creditors, such as the inability to pay wages or utility bills.

Remarks: Usually, if the current assets/current liabilities ratio is low, the cash turnover ratio will be high because of the small amount of available working capital.

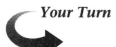

Your Turn *Answer the following:*

► *Are these ratios high or low compared to the standard?*

Standard is 9.6 times	High	Low		High	Low

$$\frac{\text{Current Assets}}{\text{Current Liabilities}} = \quad 10.7 \quad \square \quad \square \qquad 9.3 \quad \square \quad \square$$

► Which would you want in your business?

► Why?

Answers are found in Appendix D.

RATIO: DEBT TO NET WORTH

Pumping Iron Fitness Center

$$\frac{\text{Total Debt}}{\text{Net Worth}} \quad \frac{287{,}120}{26{,}980} = 10.6 \text{ times}$$

Hi-Tech Merchandise Company

$$\frac{\text{Total Debt}}{\text{Net Worth}} \quad \frac{476{,}300}{185{,}700} = 2.6 \text{ times}$$

Measures: Total debt coverage. Expresses the relationship between capital contributed by the creditors and that contributed by the owner.

Generally accepted standard: This number should be less than 80% or the creditors may want as much say as you have about the operation of your business. Some analysts think that current liabilities to net worth should not exceed 80% and long-term debt should not exceed net worth by 50%.

Low ratio means: Greater long-term financial safety, which generally means that you have greater flexibility to borrow money. An extremely low ratio may mean that the firm's management is too conservative: The firm is not reaching its full profit potential, or the profit potential from financial leverage, which is realized by borrowing money at a low rate of interest and obtaining a higher rate of return on sales.

High ratio means: Greater risk is assumed by the creditors, and they may show greater interest in the way the firm is managed. Your ability to obtain money from outside sources is limited.

Your Turn

Answer the following:

▶ *Are these ratios high or low compared to the standard?*

Standard is 60%   High Low   High Low

$$\frac{\text{Total Debt}}{\text{Net Worth}} = \quad 45\% \ \square \quad \square \qquad 35\% \ \square \quad \square$$

▶ Which would you want in your business?

▶ Why?

Answers are found in Appendix D.

Remarks: A lot depends on where the business is in its lifecycle, what the policies of the owners are, the state of the economy, your industry and the particular business cycle.

Remember, long-term debt is leverage. Leverage can work for you during the good times and against you during a sales slump. This can create fluctuating earnings if too much money is borrowed.

ANALYSIS

The current ratio for both businesses is about the same, and both are lower than the recommended two-to-one standard. Inventory is a large part of current assets. A service business such as the Pumping Iron Fitness Center usually receives its money up front before the customer uses the facility and should be in a better cash position than the retail company. However, buying and selling equipment for resale and allowing credit solidifies the liquidity. The inventory carried by the retail company is also very large, which ties up money and space. The large inventory causes accounts payable to be large, which affects liquidity, causing it to be less than what it should be. But these businesses are just starting out and are heavily financed by debt, so it will take some time for them to become more liquid.

The debts of both start-ups are high. Both debt to net worth ratios are very high but should come down as the debts are paid. The Pumping Iron Fitness Center is tied up mainly in long-term debt owing to investing in facilities and equipment. The Hi-Tech Merchandise Company appears to be in better shape; however, more than half of its debt is in current liabilities and most of these debts are in accounts payable. Hi-Tech may want to work out an arrangement with its suppliers to take longer to pay until they become better established.

Long-term debt should be properly matched to fixed assets and short-term debt should be matched to current assets or operating funds. The cash turnover ratio for the service business is much higher than it should be, which signals a possible cash crisis. However, if customers pay up front for use of the fitness facilities and if the company buys less equipment for resale or only on prepaid orders, it can get by on less working capital to support its sales volume. Since the company typically requires $14,000 – $15,000 per month in expenses, the working capital will almost meet the need.

This is not the best position to be in, but it could be worse. The Hi-Tech Merchandise Company must stock finished goods and components to customize electronic items such as computers and needs to carry the inventory and support credit sales to stay in business. To do this, a proper cash flow and working capital is necessary.

REVIEW

▶ Liquidity ratios help you determine your firm's ability to pay debts

▶ The current ratio is important, because it provides an indication of your ability to pay your immediate bills

▶ Working capital is the difference between current assets and current liabilities; it represents the amount available to pay salaries or buy new material or goods

▶ By maintaining a proper ratio for your turnover of cash, you will be able to take advantage of discounts for prompt payment

▶ Your total debt should not exceed 80% of your net worth and your long-term debt should not exceed 50% of your net worth

ASK YOURSELF

► What are the effects of financial leverage and operating leverage in long-term debt?

► How do liquidity ratios help determine a firm's ability to pay its bills?

► Define working capital.

CHAPTER
SIX

PROFITABILITY
RATIOS

Profitability is why most of us are in business. We want a better return for our money and time than we can get from a bank or other low-risk interest-paying opportunity. By the way, this comparison is one of the most commonly used methods to evaluate whether your business is doing well. For example, if savings accounts or money market accounts pay a higher percent than you earn on the money you have invested in your business, you might want to consider selling your business and reinvesting your money elsewhere unless you like your line of work better than making more money. Profitability ratios provide you with the means to measure your earnings in several ways. They measure your profit margin, return on assets, return on investment and return on sales.

As a general rule, changes in profitability or income can be the result of changes in price, volume, expenses (more salespeople or advertising), depreciation or addition of assets, or borrowing money. If you raise or lower your prices, changes will usually be shown by changes in your ratios.

The balance sheets and income statements for Pumping Iron Fitness Center and the Hi-Tech Merchandise Company will be used to demonstrate how these ratios are important to measure and control any business.

Pumping Iron Fitness Center
Balance Sheet
January 1, 19XX

Assets		Liabilities	
Current Assets		Current Liabilities	
Cash	$30,000	Accounts Payable	$20,000
Accounts Receivable	5,000	Accruals	16,000
Inventory	14,200		
Fixed Assets		Long-Term Debt	
Building	106,400	10 Year Note	173,654
Equipment/Fixtures	158,500	Mortgage	77,466
		Net Worth	26,980
Total	$314,100		$314,100

Pumping Iron Fitness Center
Income Statement
January 1, 19XX

Sales	$300,000	
Cost of Sales (Equipment)	30,000	
Gross Profit (Service)		225,00
Gross Profit (Equipment)		75,000
Total Gross Profit	270,000	

Expenses:		
Owner's Drawings	40,000	
Salaries	42,100	
Vacation/Sick Days Pay	1,130	
Health Insurance	3,900	
Unemployment Insurance	760	
Social Security Taxes	700	
Life Insurance	1,800	
Consumable Supplies	1,200	
Repairs and Maintenance	1,000	
Advertising	4,800	
Professional Expenses	1,800	
Mortgage Principal	2,534	
Loan Principal	11,346	
Telephone	3,500	
Utilities	3,600	
Insurance	3,000	
Taxes	4,560	
Interest	25,483	
Depreciation	21,960	
Miscellaneous	1,200	
Total Expenses	$176,373	
Net Profit		$93,627

Hi-Tech Merchandise Company

Balance Sheet

January 1, 19XX

Assets

Current Assets

Cash	$52,000
Accounts Receivable	185,000
Inventory	200,000

Fixed Assets

Land/Building	150,000
Equipment/Fixtures	75,000

TOTAL	$662,000

Liabilities

Current Liabilities

Notes Payable	$58,000
Accounts Payable	205,000
Accruals	46,000

Long-Term Debt

Mortgage	104,300
8 Year Note	63,000
Net Worth	185,700

TOTAL	$662,000

Hi-Tech Merchandise Company

Income Statement

January 1, 19XX

Net Sales (minus Allowances and Discounts)	$766,990
Cost of Goods Sold	560,000
Gross Profit	206,990

Expenses

Owner's Drawings	$14,000
Wages	65,000
Benefits/Social Security	7,790
Delivery	12,200
Bad Debt	4,000
Professional	2,000
Telephone	2,000
Depreciation	24,000
Repairs/Consumables	2,200
Life Insurance	1,800
Utilities	3,000
Insurance	7,000
Taxes	8,000
Interest	12,447

(continues on next page)

(continued)

Loan Principal	7,875
Mortgage Principal	2,477
Advertising	5,000
Miscellaneous	7,000
Total Expenses	187,789
Net Profit	$ 19,201

RATIO: NET PROFIT

Pumping Iron Fitness Center

$$\frac{\text{Earnings Before Interest and Taxes (EBIT)*}}{\text{Net Sales}} \quad \frac{123,670}{300,000} = 41.2\%$$

Hi-Tech Merchandise Company

$$\frac{\text{Earnings Before Interest and Taxes (EBIT)*}}{\text{Net Sales}} \quad \frac{39,684}{766,990} = 5.2\%$$

*Taxes as used here mean federal and local taxes.

Measures: The effectiveness of management. This ratio is a valid comparison between firms in the same industry; it filters any distortions that may occur because of high debt or other factors that may affect tax payment or nonpayments.

Generally accepted standard: Depends on the business or industry. The volume and age of the business are also important factors.

Low ratio means: Perhaps the business expenses or inefficiencies are too great or sales are too low for the costs.

High ratio means: There is a high earnings margin or low expenses.

Remarks: The measure of a good ratio depends on the type of business or industry, which should be compared to the industry standards. Earnings before interest and taxes (EBIT) are also called operating income. This ratio does not consider any investment made in buildings, machinery, etc.

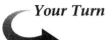

Answer the following:

▶ Interpret the following profitability ratio.

The standard is 6.7%   High   Low

$$\frac{\text{Earnings Before Interest and Taxes}}{\text{Net Sales}} = 3.4\%$$ ☐   ☐

▶ Would you want this ratio?

▶ Why or why not?

Answers are in Appendix D.

RATIO: RATE OF RETURN ON SALES

Pumping Iron Fitness Center

$$\frac{\text{Net Profit}}{\text{Net Sales}} \quad \frac{93,627}{300,000} = 31.2\%$$

Hi-Tech Merchandise Company

$$\frac{\text{Net Profit}}{\text{Net Sales}} \quad \frac{19,201}{766,990} = 2.5\%$$

Measures: How much net profit was derived from every dollar of sales. It indicates how well you have managed your operating expenses and may also indicate whether the business is generating enough sales to cover the fixed costs and still leave an acceptable profit.

Generally accepted standard: Depends on the business or industry. Price and volume are important and play a large role in determining this ratio.

Low ratio means: Not too much if you are in the right industry; for instance, one that has a high turnover of inventory or one that uses a low margin to attract business (such as a grocery store).

High ratio means: Usually the higher the ratio, the better off your business is. However, if you are beating last year's figures and show a steady increase, you are doing well.

Remarks: This ratio must be viewed with many facts in mind and used in conjunction with other ratios and analytical tools. Beware of using this ratio alone, because you may be comparing incompatible figures. Comparing it with your own results month after month or year after year is valid.

Your Turn   *Answer the following:*

▶ *Are these ratios high or low compared to the standard?*

| The standard is 4.8% | | | High | Low | | High | Low |

$$\frac{\text{Net Profit}}{\text{Net Worth}} \quad = \quad 5.6\% \ \square \quad \square \quad 5.7\% \ \square \quad \square$$

▶ Would you want the first or second ratio or both?

▶ Why?

Answers are in Appendix D.

RATIO: RATE OF RETURN ON INVESTMENT

Pumping Iron Fitness Center

$$\frac{\text{Net Profit}}{\text{Net Worth}} \quad \frac{93,627}{26,980} = 3.5 \text{ times}$$

Hi-Tech Merchandise Company

$$\frac{\text{Net Profit}}{\text{Net Worth}} \quad \frac{19,201}{185,700} = 10\%$$

Measures: Return on investment (ROI). Some use this figure as a final evaluation.

Generally accepted standard: A relationship of at least 10%–14% is considered necessary to fund future growth.

Low ratio means: Perhaps you could have done better investing your money in savings bonds or some other investment opportunity. A low ratio could indicate inefficient management performance, or it could reflect a highly capitalized, conservatively operated business.

High ratio means: Perhaps creditors were a source of much of the funds, management is efficient or the firm is undercapitalized.

Remarks: This measure is considered one of the best criteria of profitability; it can be a key ratio to compare against other firms or the industry average. However, it should be used in conjunction with other ratios. There should be a direct relationship between ROI and risk; that is, the greater the risk, the higher the return. Remember, net worth is the difference between assets and liabilities. A smaller net worth figure would equate to a higher ratio. Another measure of ROI is to add interest and taxes to net profit to get earnings before interest and taxes. This levels the playing field between start-ups and mature businesses.

Pumping Iron Fitness Center

$$\frac{\text{EBIT}}{\text{Total Assets}} = \frac{123,670}{314,100} = 39\%$$

Hi-Tech Merchandise Company

$$\frac{\text{EBIT}}{\text{Total Assets}} = \frac{39,648}{662,000} = 6\%$$

This ratio is a combination of the profitability ratio called net profit and the efficiency ratio called investment turnover, and it overcomes the shortcomings of both. But don't fail to look at each separately to tell what might have caused any changes: increased income from more sales or better utilization of your assets.

Answer the following:

▶ *Are these ratios high or low compared to the standard?*

The standard is 20%		High	Low		High	Low
$\dfrac{\text{Net Profit}}{\text{Net Sales}}$ =	12.7%	☐	☐	23.4%	☐	☐

▶ Which would you want?

▶ Why?

Answers are in Appendix D.

RATIO: RATE OF RETURN OF ASSETS

Pumping Iron Fitness Center

$$\frac{\text{Net Profit}}{\text{Total Assets}} \quad \frac{93,627}{314,100} = 29\%$$

Hi-Tech Merchandise Company

$$\frac{\text{Net Profit}}{\text{Total Assets}} \quad \frac{19,201}{662,000} = 3\%$$

Measures: The profit that is generated by the use of the assets of the business.

Generally accepted standard: Varies depending on the industry and the amount of fixed assets that must be used, the amount of cash that must be available, etc.

Low ratio means: Poor performance or ineffective employment of the assets by management.

High ratio means: Good performance or effective use of the firm's assets by its management.

Remarks: This ratio can easily be distorted by a heavily depreciated plant, a large amount of intangible assets, or unusual income or expense items. This ratio should be used with other ratios to compare firms in the same industry and of approximately the same size. It is a valid tool if you know the real value of your competitor's assets (especially fixed assets) and whether your competitors include outside earnings as a large part of their current assets. If you don't know, beware of making a firm conclusion from this ratio alone.

A variation of this ratio is to split the assets into fixed and current and work a ratio on each of them. Knowing the return on fixed assets could be important to a business that has to count on a heavy investment in fixed assets, such as rolling stock or heavy machinery, to generate sales and profits.

Your Turn

Answer the following:

▶ *Are these ratios high or low compared to the standard?*

The standard is 5%

		High	Low		High	Low
$\dfrac{\text{Net Profit}}{\text{Net Sales}} =$	23%	☐	☐	7.8%	☐	☐

▶ Which is better?

▶ Why?

Answers are in Appendix D.

ANALYSIS OF THE PROFITABILITY RATIOS

The Pumping Iron Fitness Center's earnings before interest and taxes to net sales are higher than industry's. This may indicate a good use of assets, except that the liquidity ratios are low and so is working capital, so probably most of the "profit" is not in cash. If some cash is available, it should be used to reduce debt. If the earnings keep growing, the debt and liquidity problem should be minimal.

Net profit on sales is in line with the EBIT, which indicates that the interest and local taxes are not excessive for this industry. Net profit to net worth indicates the effect of financial leverage, because the owners borrowed heavily to start the business.

When sales are good this reflects a healthy business, but if sales fall repayment of the note can be a heavy burden.

Net profit to total assets indicate that the fitness center is way above the industry average. Compare this ratio to the one for EBIT to total assets, which shows a dramatic jump in the ratio when the interest expense is added to net profit, which shows what is possible when the interest payments are lower.

The Hi-Tech Merchandise Company's EBIT to net sales ratio and net profit to net sales ratio are very close to the industry's, but the company still has debt and liquidity problems. Net profit to net worth is quite low compared to the industry standard but should improve as debts are lowered and cash flow improves.

Net profit to total assets shows that the assets aren't fully employed, but this is a start-up business and things should get better. When interest and local taxes are subtracted, this percentage doubles but is still short of the standard. This problem can be helped by getting expenses in line and generating more sales with the same assets.

REVIEW

- ► Profitability ratios measure profit margin, return on assets, return on investment and return on sales

- ► Profitability is a result of several things such as your price structure, the amount of business you do and how well you control your expenses

- ► The net profit ratio is a valid ratio to measure your business to your industry average

- ► Your return on investment can be measured as a return on net worth or total assets

- ► The rate of return on sales must be used with caution when comparing your business with other businesses

- ► Beware of using the rate of return on total assets ratio to compare your business with others without knowing the condition of the fixed assets, if the fixed assets are leased and if outside earnings are a part of current assets

ASK YOURSELF

► Describe how profitability ratios help to measure earnings.

► How does a change in pricing or volume affect profitability ratios?

► Why, as a general rule, is a high ratio preferred for the rate of return on sales?

► What is the relationship between risk and return on investment (ROI)?

► How can the rate of return on assets ratio be distorted by a heavily depreciated plant?

CHAPTER
SEVEN

EFFICIENCY
RATIOS

Efficiency ratios measure how well you conduct your business. These ratios indicate how fast you are collecting your money for credit sales and how many times you turn over your inventory in a given period of time. They measure the amount of sales generated by and the return you are earning on your assets. Efficiency ratios are an important landmark in situating your business. For instance, if you become too loose in offering credit to generate sales, this carelessness will show up as an increase in the average number of days it takes to collect your accounts receivable. If you overbuy, even if you can't pass up a real bargain, this enthusiasm will be reflected in a decrease in the turnover of your inventory. If you acquire too many fixed assets without a corresponding increase in sales, this ratio will quickly remind you of lower sales generated by your assets. Of course, other ratios that will aid you in achieving a healthy growth also play a part in maintaining a balance in your business, but the efficiency ratios will usually note it sooner.

All ratios will be developed and analyzed from the balance sheets and income statements, for the Pumping Iron Fitness Center and the Hi-Tech Merchandise Company. The efficiency ratios will pertain to almost all new businesses, whether it was started from scratch or bought as an existing business. Notice that some efficiency ratios are expressed in days and not percentages or proportions.

Pumping Iron Fitness Center
Balance Sheet
January 1, 19XX

Assets		Liabilities	
Current Assets		Current Liabilities	
Cash	$30,000	Accounts Payable	$20,000
Accounts Receivable	5,000	Accruals	16,000
Inventory	14,200		
Fixed Assets		Long-Term Debt	
Building	106,400	10 Year Note	173,654
Equipment/Fixtures	158,500	Mortgage	77,466
		Net Worth	26,980
Total	$314,100		$314,100

Pumping Iron Fitness Center
Income Statement
January 1, 19XX

Sales	$300,000	
Cost of Sales (equipment)	30,000	
Gross Profit (service)		225,000
Gross Profit (equipment)		75,000
Total Gross Profit	270,000	
Expenses:		
Owner's Drawings	40,000	
Salaries	42,100	
Vacation/Sick Days Pay	1,130	
Health Insurance	3,900	
Unemployment Insurance	760	
Social Security Taxes	700	
Life Insurance	1,800	
Consumable Supplies	1,200	
Repairs and Maintenance	1,000	
Advertising	4,800	
Professional Expenses	1,800	
Mortgage Principal	2,534	
Loan Principal	11,346	
Telephone	3,500	
Utilities	3,600	
Insurance	3,000	
Taxes	4,560	
Interest	25,483	
Depreciation	21,960	
Miscellaneous	1,200	
Total Expenses	$176,373	
Net Profit		$93,627

Hi-Tech Merchandise Company

Balance Sheet

January 1, 19XX

Assets		Liabilities	
Current Assets		**Current Liabilities**	
Cash	$52,000	Notes Payable	$58,000
Accounts Receivable	185,000	Accounts Payable	205,000
Inventory	200,000	Accruals	46,000
Fixed Assets		**Long-Term Debt**	
Land/Building	150,000	Mortgage	104,300
Equipment/Fixtures	75,000	8 Year Note	63,000
		Net Worth	185,700
TOTAL	$662,000	TOTAL	$662,000

Hi-Tech Merchandise Company

Income Statement

January 1, 19XX

Net Sales (minus allowances and discounts)	$766,990
(Credit sales $575,300)	
Cost of Goods Sold	560,000
Gross Profit	206,990

Expenses

Owner's Drawings	$14,000
Wages	65,000
Benefits/Social Security	7,790
Delivery	12,200
Bad Debt	4,000
Professional	2,000
Telephone	2,000
Depreciation	24,000
Repairs/Consumables	2,200
Life Insurance	1,800
Utilities	3,000

(continues on next page)

(continued)

Insurance	7,000
Taxes	8,000
Interest	12,447
Loan Principal	7,875
Mortgage Principal	2,477
Advertising	5,000
Miscellaneous	7,000

Total Expenses	187,789	
Net Profit		$19,201

RATIO: AVERAGE COLLECTION PERIOD FOR ACCOUNTS RECEIVABLE

Pumping Iron Fitness Center

$$\frac{\text{Accounts Receivable} \times 365 \text{ Days/Year}}{\text{Credit Sales}} = \frac{5,000 \times 365}{42,600} = 42.8 \text{ days}$$

Hi-Tech Merchandise Company

$$\frac{\text{Accounts Receivable} \times 365 \text{ Days/Year}}{\text{Credit Sales}} = \frac{185,000 \times 365}{575,000} = 117.4 \text{ days}$$

Measures: The turnover of receivables. The average period of time it takes to collect your credit sales dollars.

Generally accepted standard: Depends on your collection period policy—if it is 30 days, then 30 days is the standard.

Low ratio means: A slow turnover, which may be the result of bad accounts, a lax collection policy or, perhaps, credit that is used to generate sales.

High ratio means: A fast turnover, which could be the result of a stringent collection policy or fast-paying customers.

Remarks: Generally anything within 10–15 days of *your* collection period is deemed acceptable and considered within the collection period.

Another variation is a two-step process that first measures your average daily credit sales and then provides the average collection period. If average daily credit sales are important, use the following ratio. If not, the average collection period for accounts receivable is easier and quicker to use. Both provide the same answer.

Pumping Iron Fitness Center

$$\frac{\text{Net Credit Sales}}{365} = \frac{42,600}{365} = \$117 = \text{Daily Credit Sales}$$

$$\frac{\text{Accounts Receivable}}{\text{Daily Credit Sales}} = \frac{5,000}{117} = 42.7 \text{ Days} = \begin{array}{c} \text{Average} \\ \text{Collection Period} \end{array}$$

Hi-Tech Merchandise Company

$$\frac{\text{Net Credit Sales}}{365} = \frac{575,300}{365} = \$1,576 = \text{Daily Credit Sales}$$

$$\frac{\text{Accounts Receivable}}{\text{Daily Credit Sales}} = \frac{185,000}{1,576} = 117.3 \text{ Days} = \begin{array}{c} \text{Average} \\ \text{Collection Period} \end{array}$$

Your Turn

Answer the following:

► *Is this ratio high or low compared to the standard?*

The standard is 35 days   High   Low

$$\frac{\text{Accounts Receivable x 365 Days/Year}}{\text{Credit Sales}} = 35 \text{ Days} \quad \square \quad \square$$

► Would you want this average collection period of time?

► Why?

Answers are in Appendix D.

RATIO: INVENTORY TURNOVER (STOCK TO SALES RATIO)

Pumping Iron Fitness Center

$$\frac{\text{Cost of Goods Sold}}{\text{Average Inventory}} \quad \frac{30,000}{14,200} = 2.1 \text{ times}$$

(173 DOH)*

or

$$\frac{\text{Net Sales}}{\text{Average Inventory}} \quad \frac{300,000}{14,200} = 21 \text{ times}$$

(17 DOH)*

Hi-Tech Merchandise Company

$$\frac{\text{Cost of Goods Sold}}{\text{Average Inventory}} \quad \frac{560,000}{200,000} = 2.8 \text{ times}$$

(130 DOH)*

or

$$\frac{\text{Net Sales}}{\text{Average Inventory}} \quad \frac{766,990}{200,000} = 3.8 \text{ times}$$

(96 DOH)*

*DOH = days on hand (see remarks)

The cost of goods sold figure is used by some analysts because most inventories are carried on the balance sheet by how much they cost, not the selling price, which is shown by using net sales. (Note the distortion between cost of goods sold and net sales for the service company. This happens when little inventory is carried.)

Note: Manufacturers inventory = finished goods, raw material and in-process material.

Measures: Inventory turnover. This ratio shows how fast your merchandise is moving; that is, how many times your initial inventory is replaced in a month/year.

Generally accepted standard: Depends on the industry and even the time of year for some industries. However, six–seven times is a rule of thumb.

Low ratio means: An indication of a large inventory, a never-out-of-stock situation, perhaps some obsolete items—or it could indicate poor liquidity, some possible overstocking of items or a planned buildup in anticipation of a coming high-selling period.

High ratio means: An indication of a narrow selection, maybe fast-moving merchandise or perhaps some lost sales. It may indicate better liquidity, maybe superior merchandising or a shortage of inventory needed for sales.

Remarks: Faster turnovers are generally viewed as a positive trend: They increase cash flow and reduce warehousing. This ratio measures how management uses inventory and can be used to compare one period to the next or to another company in the same industry or the industry average.

This ratio is an indicator, not an absolute measure or count. A small retail business should not carry more than 100% of its working capital in inventory.

*To determine days on hand (DOH), divide the inventory turnover (IT) ratio into 365 days:

$$\frac{365}{IT} = \text{the average number of days the inventory is on hand.}$$

$$\frac{365}{3.8} = 96 \text{ days on hand}$$

Answer the following:

▶ **Is this ratio high or low compared to the standard?**

The standard is 5.5 times   High Low   High Low

$$\frac{\text{Cost of Goods Sold}}{\text{Average Inventory}} = 5 \text{ times} \quad \square \quad \square \quad 7 \text{ times} \quad \square \quad \square$$

▶ Which would you want?

▶ Why?

Answers are in Appendix D.

RATIO: FIXED ASSETS TO NET WORTH

Pumping Iron Fitness Center

$$\frac{\text{Fixed Assets}}{\text{Net Worth}} \quad \frac{264,900}{26,980} = 9.8 \text{ times}$$

Hi-Tech Merchandise Company

$$\frac{\text{Fixed Assets}}{\text{Net Worth}} \quad \frac{225,000}{185,700} = 1.2 \text{ times}$$

Measures: The amount of fixed assets that are a part of net worth. This ratio is important because it provides an indication of how much capital is tied up in low-liquid assets.

Generally accepted standard: A rule of thumb for small business is that not more than 75% of your net worth should be tied up in fixed assets. If fixed assets are approaching 75% of the firm's net worth, the firm may need working capital to meet current expenses.

Low ratio means: A smaller investment in fixed assets in relation to net worth; that is, net worth may consist of more liquid assets. This situation is better for creditors.

High ratio means: A larger investment in plant and property, which may be harder to liquidate if cash is needed, especially if they are not paid for.

Remarks: Fixed assets should be carried on the balance sheet as depreciated fixed assets, not original cost. The presence of substantial leased fixed assets (those not shown on a balance sheet) may deceptively lower this ratio. The amount of fixed assets depends on the industry: for example, the fixed asset requirement for a trucking company or a heavy equipment operating business may be relatively high, but it will be low for an average retailer or consultant.

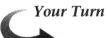 **Your Turn**   ***Answer the following:***

► **Is this ratio high or low compared to the standard?**

		High	Low		High	Low
The standard is 65%						

$$\frac{\text{Fixed Assets}}{\text{Net worth}} = \quad 75\% \ \square \quad \square \qquad 55\% \ \square \quad \square$$

► Which is usually better?

► Why?

Answers are in Appendix D.

RATIO: INVESTMENT TURNOVER

Pumping Iron Fitness Center

$$\frac{\text{Net Sales}}{\text{Total Assets}} \quad \frac{300,000}{314,100} = 95.5\%$$

Hi-Tech Merchandise Company

$$\frac{\text{Net Sales}}{\text{Total Assets}} \quad \frac{766,990}{662,000} = 1.2 \text{ times}$$

Measures: Ability of the firm to generate sales in relation to assets.

Generally accepted standard: Varies greatly depending on the business and the industry; for instance, a service business has low fixed assets and little, if any, inventory compared to a manufacturing company.

Low ratio means: The assets may not be fully employed, or too many assets may be chasing too few sales. The assets are not pulling their own weight. The firm may be expanding but the business is not growing.

High ratio means: More sales may be generated with fewer assets, which may indicate that something good is happening or has happened. Maybe you are getting more sales from the same buildings and equipment.

Remarks: This ratio should be used only to compare firms within specific industry groups and in conjunction with other ratios. As with any ratio measuring assets, it can give a distorted reading if the assets are heavily depreciated or if there is a large amount of intangible assets such as goodwill. When comparing two firms or comparing with the industry averages, be careful that the asset figures are approximately the same. This ratio does not consider a price increase or decrease or how well you watch your expenses. This ratio, when combined with the net profit ratio becomes another return on investment (ROI) ratio.

Another version is:

Pumping Iron Fitness Center

$$\frac{\text{Net Sales}}{\text{Fixed Assets}} = \frac{300,000}{264,900} = 1.1 \text{ times}$$

Hi-Tech Merchandise Company

$$\frac{\text{Net Sales}}{\text{Fixed Assets}} = \frac{766,990}{225,000} = 3.4 \text{ times}$$

This version is important if your business requires a large investment in fixed assets.

The standard is 4 times   High   Low   High   Low

$$\frac{\text{Net Sales}}{\text{Total Assets}} = 1.8 \text{ times} \quad \square \quad \square \qquad 5 \text{ times} \quad \square \quad \square$$

▶ Which is usually better?

▶ Why?

Answers are in Appendix D.

An analysis of the efficiency ratios for the Pumping Iron Fitness Center shows that accounts receivable are above a 30-day standard. This situation will not get the center into serious trouble, but the company should institute a policy for payment and stick by it. The extra collection could be used to reduce debt.

Inventory turnover is a difficult ratio to compare, because the industry has few hardware sales or deals only in cash. Compared to the turnover of a sporting-goods store, however, the turnover of the Pumping Iron Fitness Center is very low.

Because it is a start-up business with heavy borrowing, the fixed assets are about all there is to net worth. This ratio should improve with steady or increasing sales and declining expenses. Now the ratio is too high. Net sales to assets are also low, meaning the assets are not fully employed and can support more sales. If the center attracts new customers and retains the old, this ratio will improve; if not, some assets should be sold, because they do not support sufficient sales. The net sales to fixed assets ratio shows that fixed assets is the biggest contributor to the low net sales to assets ratio.

In the case of the Hi-Tech Merchandise Company, accounts receivable is a large part of sales. The collection rate needs improving, which would improve the cash and debt position of the company. The owner might want to examine the qualifying criteria for credit.

The cost-of-goods-sold turnover is quite low; weeding out slow-moving merchandise will improve that ratio. More sales also will help, but increased sales conflict with tighter credit sales and improved credit collecting. The owner must find a better middle ground to keep the business in balance.

This is a start-up business and, as expected, fixed assets are a large part of net worth. If this situation does not improve in time; that is, if sales do not increase, fixed assets should be reduced. The ratios of net sales to total assets and to fixed assets are also low, as might be expected with a start-up, which also indicates that more sales can be supported with the same amount of assets, especially fixed assets.

REVIEW

- ► Efficiency ratios measure how well you conduct your business

- ► Efficiency ratios help keep your business in balance

- ► Your accounts receivable times 365 days then divided by your credit sales will tell you how long it takes for your average customer to pay a bill

- ► Dividing your cost of goods sold by your average inventory gives you the number of times you replace your inventory per month or per year

- ► To find out the amount of fixed assets that are a part of your net worth, divide your fixed assets by your net worth

- ► Your net sales divided by your total assets tells you how well you generate sales in relation to your total assets

- ► A variation of the above ratio substitutes fixed assets for total assets to see how well you generate sales in relation to your fixed assets.

ASK YOURSELF

▶ What can you learn from efficiency ratios?

▶ Describe the inventory turnover ratio—what does it include and what does it measure?

▶ How does the accounts receivable turnover ratio relate to the cash flow of the business?

▶ Describe the return on assets ratio and what it measures.

▶ Why is the return on investment one of the best ratios for comparing your business with another in your industry?

CHAPTER
EIGHT

RATIO
ANALYSIS

EVALUATE THE DATA

Ratios are more than isolated figures. When they are organized cohesively, they become a powerful tool in your business analysis. This section presents forms and charts that will help you collect, organize and evaluate your business through the use of the ratio review chart.

DATA COLLECTION CHARTS

The next two forms will help you organize your ratios and use the ratio review chart. The data gathering form provides a means of gathering the figures from the balance sheet and income statement. The comparison chart provides spaces to work your ratios and insert your industry averages.

The industry average figures are compiled by several companies (for a partial listing, see Appendix A). This information may be bought from these sources, but it is usually available through a banker, public or university library, small business association office or the Chamber of Commerce. Your trade association may also compile these statistics, and if they are regional, they may be more appropriate for your use.

To make the best use of these charts, copy them and fill in the blanks from your balance sheet and income statement. Examples are provided; the ratio comparison chart shows how they are used. All the information has been taken from the balance sheets and income statements of the hypothetical Pumping Iron Fitness Center and Hi-Tech Merchandise Company. Blank pages that you may use for your own business are included.

DATA GATHERING FORM

Business Name: Pumping Iron Fitness Center

Business Address: Anywhere U.S.A.

Date Prepared: XX/YY/ZZ

Items	Dollar Figures
Current Assets	$49,200
Current Liabilities	$36,000
Net Sales	$300,000
Working Capital	$13,200
Total Debt	$287,120
Net Worth	$26,980
Earnings Before Interest and Taxes	$123,670
Net Profit	$93,627
Total Assets	$314,100
Accounts Receivable	$5,000
Costs of Goods Sold	$30,000
Average Inventory	$14,200
Fixed Assets	$264,900
Credit Sales	$42,600

DATA GATHERING FORM

Business Form: Hi-Tech Merchandise Company

Business Address: Anywhere U.S.A.

Date Prepared: XX/YY/ZZ

Items	Dollar Figures
Current Assets	$437,000
Current Liabilities	$309,000
Net Sales	$766,990
Working Capital	$128,000
Total Debt	$476,300
Net Worth	$185,700
Earnings Before Interest and Taxes	$39,648
Net Profit	$19,201
Total Assets	$662,000
Accounts Receivable	$185,000
Cost of Goods Sold	$560,000
Average Inventory	$200,000
Fixed Assets	$225,000
Credit Sales	$575,000

COMPARISON CHART

Business Name: Pumping Iron Fitness Center

Business Address: Anywhere U.S.A.

Date Prepared: XX/YY/ZZ

Ratios	Dollar Figures	My Ratios	Industry Averages
Current Assets / Current Liabilities	$49,200 / $36,000	1.4 Times	2.1 Times
Sales / Working Capital	$300,000 / $13,200	22.7 Times	8.7 Times
Total Debt / Net Worth	$278,120 / $26,980	10.3 Times	60%
Earnings Before Interest and Taxes / Net Sales	$123,670 / $300,000	41.2%	39.5%
Net Profit / Net Sales	$93,627 / $300,000	31.2%	30.1%
Net Profit / Net Worth	$93,627 / $26,980	3.5 Times	40.2%
Net Profit / Total Assets	$93,627 / $314,100	29.8%	28.1%
Accounts Receivable × 365 / Sales (credit)	$5,500 × 365 / $42,600	47.1 Days	23 Days
Cost of Goods Sold / Average Inventory	$30,000 / $14,200	2.1 Times	N/A
Fixed Assets / Net Worth	$264,900 / $26,980	9.8 Times	30%
Net Sales / Total Assets	$300,000 / $314,100	95.5%	2.2 Times
Net Sales / Fixed Assets	$300,000 / $264,900	1.1 Times	5.5 Times

Note: Industry averages are for example only.

COMPARISON CHART

Business Name: Hi-Tech Merchandise Company

Business Address: Anywhere U.S.A.

Date Prepared: XX/YY/ZZ

Ratios	Dollar Figures	My Ratios	Industry Averages
Current Assets / Current Liabilities	$437,000 / $309,000	1.4 Times	1.8 Times
Sales / Working Capital	$766,990 / $128,000	6 Times	8.9 Times
Total Debt / Net Worth	$476,300 / $185,700	2.6 Times	1.8 Times
Earnings Before Interest and Taxes / Net Sales	$31,684 / $766,990	4.1%	3.8%
Net Profit / Net Sales	$19,201 / $766,990	2.5%	2.9%
Net Profit / Net Worth	$19,201 / $185,700	10%	30.1%
Net Profit / Total Assets	$19,201 / $622,000	3%	15.1%
Accounts Receivable × 365 / Sales (credit)	$185,000 × 365 / $575,000	117.4 Days	39 Days
Cost of Goods Sold / Average Inventory	$560,000 / $200,000	2.8 Times	11.8 Times
Fixed Assets / Net Worth	$225,000 / $185,700	1.2 Times	30%
Net Sales / Total Assets	$766,990 / $662,000	1.2 Times	4.4 Times
Net Sales / Fixed Assets	$766,990 / $225,000	3.4 Times	11.6 Times

Note: Industry averages are for example only.

DATA GATHERING FORM

Business Name: _____

Business Address: _____

Date Prepared: _____

Items	Dollar Figures
Current Assets	
Current Liabilities	
Net Sales	
Working Capital	
Total Debt	
Net Worth	
Earnings Before Interest and Taxes	
Net Profit	
Total Assets	
Accounts Receivable	
Cost of Goods Sold	
Average Inventory	
Fixed Assets	
Total Assets	

COMPARISON CHART

Business Name: _____

Business Address: _____

Date Prepared: _____

Ratios	Dollar Figures	My Ratios	Industry Averages
$\dfrac{\text{Current Assets}}{\text{Current Liabilities}}$	_____		
$\dfrac{\text{Sales}}{\text{Working Capital}}$	_____		
$\dfrac{\text{Total Debt}}{\text{Net Worth}}$	_____		
$\dfrac{\text{Earnings Before Interest and Taxes}}{\text{Net Sales}}$	_____		
$\dfrac{\text{Net Profit}}{\text{Net Sales}}$	_____		
$\dfrac{\text{Net Profit}}{\text{Net Worth}}$	_____		
$\dfrac{\text{Net Profit}}{\text{Total Assets}}$	_____		
$\dfrac{\text{Accounts Receivable} \times 365}{\text{Sales (credit)}}$	_____		
$\dfrac{\text{Cost of Goods Sold}}{\text{Average Inventory}}$	_____		
$\dfrac{\text{Fixed Assets}}{\text{Net Worth}}$	_____		
$\dfrac{\text{Net Sales}}{\text{Total Assets}}$	_____		
$\dfrac{\text{Net Sales}}{\text{Fixed Assets}}$	_____		

The following ratio review chart should help stimulate your thinking by indicating areas of success and areas that need improvement. However, it cannot provide all the answers.

To use the chart most efficiently, make several copies and complete one each month with your ratios. Please note that your industry averages will usually be published quarterly, so you may not have them for a month-to-month comparison. However, quick comparisons can be made and progress can be charted to help keep your business in balance. Furthermore, the chart does not consider the age of your business, the time of the business cycle, local or national economic conditions or any specific mixes of business, which should be included when you analyze your business. Last, the page number of each ratio is listed as an aid.

Remember, things take time. Don't try for too big a correction, because it may cause problems in other areas.

RATIO REVIEW CHART

Ratio	Your Ratio	Ind Avg*	If My Ratio Is High	If My Ratio Is Low
Current Assets / Current Liabilities			Check your debt, savings accounts, inventory, etc., to see that your money is working for you	Check inventory, accounts receivable and debt structure to see if you can obtain more cash
Sales / Working Capital			Check the ratio above; see if you can obtain more cash	You may have a cash surplus; invest it in the business, savings or pay debts
Total Debt / Net Worth			Check current and long-term debt structure	If too low, consider borrowing if the payback is right
EBIT / Net Sales			Keep up the good work	See below ratio for effect of interest/taxes
Net Profit / Net Sales			Keep up the good work	Check expenses and sales expectations
Net Profit / Net Worth			Check your net worth structure; you could be undercapitalized or a good manager	Check your debt structure, expenses or operating policies
Net Profit / Total Assets			Keep up the good work	Check your operating policy for asset use
Accounts Receivable × 365 / Sales (credit)			Keep up the good work	Check your credit policy
Cost of Goods Sold / Average Inventory			Could be a good sign; check inventory and unfilled sales orders	Check for overstocking or obsolete items; check cash flow
Fixed Assets / Net Worth			Check necessity of fixed assets	Depends on your type of business
Net Sales / Total Assets			Keep up the good work	Check necessity for all assets; check if sales can't be increased

WHAT'S SIGNIFICANT

To determine which ratios to use, consider the type of business you have, its age, the point in the business cycle and what you are looking for. For instance, your business might require a large number of fixed assets: buildings, land, equipment and tools. The significant ratios would certainly be those that help you measure how well you are using the fixed assets; that is, the rate of return on fixed assets.

Another business may need to carry a well-stocked inventory or just enough to satisfy emergency needs, because customers will wait for more costly items to be delivered. In either case, your inventory turnover becomes critical, and if it gets too far out of hand you may not be able to pay current expenses or have the stock to satisfy your customers.

The age of your business is important. If you have passed the initial three to five years start-up and achieved liquidity, you probably are interested in expanding or obtaining more for your investment. In this case you will want to monitor the profitability and efficiency ratios. Be careful to keep your business operations in balance.

Some businesses depend on seasonality for their income. That is, more business is done during one or more periods of the year than any other. During each rise and fall of this cycle the ratios will be quite different. It becomes necessary to watch these times so that your ratios reflect what is needed. Thus, if you expect to have a big sale or a low sales period, you will need liquidity to carry you through. If you have sold on credit, you will need to keep up a reasonable collection time between the sale and the payment or you may face a lack of working capital. If you plan to expand, you will want to be able to show a continuous profit in line with your industry and a low debt structure to influence lenders to provide you with the money you need at a favorable interest rate.

Ratios are good tools to analyze a business, but they are not entirely predictable. A rule of thumb states that if one ratio goes up, another comes down, but ratios generally don't work out so neatly. Sometimes two or more ratios indicate good work, but both are high. Sometimes, depending on your business or the time in your business cycle, it won't make any difference what a ratio does because it doesn't particularly affect you.

The proper use of ratios also considers the economy, business cycle and whether your business is just getting started, is achieving growth or has reached maturity. Improperly using ratios can worsen your position. However, ratios are only one technique of many that help you keep your business in balance. It is important to remember that all the tools will not be used all the time.

Your Turn

Interpret these ratios.

	Ratio	My Ratio	Industrial Average
1.	$\dfrac{\text{Current Assets}}{\text{Current Liabilities}}$	1.26 times	1.6 times
2.	$\dfrac{\text{Sales}}{\text{Working Capital}}$	7.06 times	14.9 times
3.	$\dfrac{\text{Total Debt}}{\text{Net Worth}}$	80%	73%
4.	$\dfrac{\text{Accounts Receivable} \times 365}{\text{Credit Sales}}$	48.6 days	32 days
5.	$\dfrac{\text{Net Sales}}{\text{Total Assets}}$	11.4 times	12.2 times
6.	$\dfrac{\text{Net Profit}}{\text{Net Sales}}$	8.1%	6.7%

Possible interpretations are in Appendix D.

REVIEW

► The first step in determining the interaction between ratios is to record the proper dollar figures from your balance sheet and income statement

► Then transfer the dollar figures from the data gathering form to the comparison chart, then determine your ratios and place them on the chart

► Third, look up your industry ratio averages and place them on the chart

► Last, compare how your ratios match up with those of your industry; then plan how to improve your weaker elements

► The ratio review chart provides a quick means of determining what corrective action you should take

► All ratios will not be significant to you all the time

► Ratios will react differently depending on the age and type of your business, the time in the business cycle and economic conditions

ASK YOURSELF

Ask yourself the following:

▶ Why is gathering balance sheet and income statement data important?

▶ Discuss the rationale for using industry averages, rather than setting your own standard.

▶ Explain why keeping your business in balance is important.

CHAPTER
NINE

EXPENSE ANALYSIS

RE-EXAMINE YOUR EXPENSES

Control of expenses begins with a well thought-out budget that is made at least once a year. The thought and homework that went into your pro-forma analysis is what must be put into your budget, which will be in the form of the pro-forma statement when you finish. The detailed notes that went into the final figures can then be worked into a detailed planned budget for each week, month and year depending on how much control you need. To project sales, look ahead into next year and beyond to see what you can reasonably expect. Next examine your past expenses.

By examining your past and current expenses, you can minimize unwarranted increases or unexpected surges and realize greater profits on the same or fewer sales. A good examination begins with sales at the top of your income statement. By understanding why sales did or did not occur as planned, you will be in a better position to project future sales and understand whether increases or decreases of expenses were justified. First, note if any extraordinary events, such as an unusually large sale to one or more customers skewed the sales figures. Perhaps what should have been a slow month became a steady one for sales. Perhaps the weather or road construction was a factor. If inventory is replaced as sales are made, and some incident caused sales to rise temporarily, buyers might have overstocked, which prompted price reductions and an overall loss of profit for the year.

Sales is a function of price times volume. Therefore, an increase in either will increase sales and a decrease in either will decrease sales. Marking down the price for a planned sale and not increasing volume sufficiently to offset the markdown will result in a loss of profit, other things being equal. If you had planned to take a trade discount because you bought more for a sale or as a normal business practice and money wasn't available to pay in time to take the discount, then when the merchandise arrived and the customers didn't, there could be double trouble.

THE COST OF GOODS SOLD

The next item under sales on the income statement is usually the cost of goods sold. Check to see if there has been an increase or a decrease. Look at possible causes such as items that increased or decreased in price, trade discounts that were not taken or allowed or something else—increased freight charges, spoilage or "shrinkage" (theft, breakage). An examination of the cost of goods sold should consider all the factors that are a part of it. A good review may include comparing invoices with past charges for the same merchandise.

This area may seem a "so what—it takes money to make money" sort of philosophy. But money can be made by paying attention and sweating the details. It does cost money to make money. The trick is to shorten the time between commitment of cash and the collection of cash. One of the ways is to review expenses continually.

Let's move on to fixed expenses, which may include rent, interest, insurance, depreciation, taxes and licenses. Each fixed expense should be the same monthly cost for the whole year. Thus, an increase in sales should cause the profit margin to increase faster than if the costs were all variable; that is, profits increase as sales increase. The reverse is true if sales decrease and expenses can't be reduced. This is another form of leverage.

Control of expenses, especially fixed expenses, should include:

▶ Negotiating the best price for the services at the beginning

▶ Bartering

▶ Paying only as much and as often as you have to, continually looking for better prices

▶ Never paying early but not late enough to miss a discount

▶ Assuming that all payment terms are negotiable

▶ Investing—not spending—depreciation

Next check variable expenses, which may include salaries, advertising, delivery, supplies, dues and subscriptions, telephone and utilities. These costs should be analyzed in relation to return on sales. They are comparable with the "year to date" figures and percentages. These percentages should compare with industry guide percentages and your past experience. If sales rise or fall and these percentages do not follow, closer examination is necessary.

Do not assume that all expenses are bad. Your expense figure is a good place to look for trends, and remember that balance is necessary. Lower expenses do not necessarily mean higher profits in the long run.

By analyzing the variable expenses, you can determine their value in relation to creating sales or increasing margin. This evaluation is vital in forecasting expenses and planning for new product lines, a sale or an expansion. If sales are slow, expenses may be adjusted accordingly.

At the bottom of the statement is net profit. Net profit might match industry standards, but other variables can still cause trouble. For example, low expenses may offset low profit margins. If some expense items were reduced and the profit margin did not rise, then something offset the anticipated gain. This situation indicates that there may be trouble elsewhere, such as in the cost of goods sold or poor sales. Remember that it's collected dollars, not sales dollars, that you take to the bank. Don't confuse profits with cash flow.

WHAT TO DO WHEN THERE IS NO MORE ROOM TO CUT

When all costs have been cut and there appears to be nothing else that can be done, try increasing the return on your expenses.

This can be done in several ways:

1. Examine your credit policy

- ▶ Invoice promptly
- ▶ Provide clear and understandable information concerning any terms and collection policy
- ▶ Maintain a receivables aging schedule and a prompt follow-up on delinquent customers
- ▶ Check credit references or make your customers think you do
- ▶ Determine if offering discounts for fast payment will help you

2. Examine your cash pay-outs

- ► Take advantage of trade discounts

- ► Pay each bill only as soon as you have to. Do not set up a "bill pay day" each month and possibly forfeit discounts for some and pay early to others

- ► If you are having a temporary cash flow problem, try to establish advantageous extended terms with creditors such as extended dating (where the 2/10, net 30 will begin in 60 days) or by paying a certain percentage of the debt over a long period of time; however, don't take over-advantage of your creditors.

- ► Buy only what is needed—when it is needed (just-in-time inventory control)

3. Examine your payroll

- ► Before hiring new employees consider overtime, part-time, temporary, freelance and outsourced labor

- ► Don't pay all your employees on the same day

- ► Examine your salary or drawings for reduction during slack periods and increase them during higher volume times

- ► Check amount of machine downtime

- ► Check starting and quitting times

- ► Check length of break times and personal times

- ► Check petty cash flow

- ► Be careful of providing too many employee benefits; they are quite expensive and uncontrollable

4. Examine your inventory controls

- ► Check your security protection to prevent theft

- ► Instruct your employees in proper handling and storing to prevent breakage and damage to inventory

- ► Be sure you have included the cost of inventory, storage, handling, insurance, taxes, deterioration, obsolescence, etc., then check the turnover rate to see if the inventory can be reduced

- ▶ Look into just-in-time inventory
- ▶ Don't be caught with obsolete inventory

5. Examine your manufacturing plans

- ▶ Look into using contractors
- ▶ Look into using "cottage industry" contractors
- ▶ Tighten up planning and scheduling
- ▶ Whatever you do—do quality work—because rework can be really costly

6. Examine your marketing plans

- ▶ Be careful to reach your specific trade area
- ▶ Have a clear policy on returns and repairs
- ▶ If discounts are offered, be sure they will work and have a way to end them if they don't work
- ▶ Train salespeople to suggest accessory items
- ▶ Provide good service and be courteous to your customers
- ▶ Train those employees who work directly with your customers, even if these employees are minimum wage employees. First impressions can gain or lose business.

7. Examine your purchasing costs

- ▶ Reduce the number of items purchased
- ▶ Reduce the number of vendors
- ▶ Eliminate unprofitable products
- ▶ Reduce the number of parts required to make your product
- ▶ Look at the overall costs, not just the purchase price
- ▶ Don't sacrifice quality for low prices unintentionally
- ▶ Work for a good relationship with your vendors

8. Other areas to examine

- ▶ Use customer-furnished material
- ▶ Avoid unnecessary extras, such as store improvements

▶ Avoid unnecessary volume purchases

▶ Keep good records

▶ Barter

▶ Make cash deposits daily and invest any surplus

▶ When you think you have covered it all—do it again

Your Turn   ***Answer these questions from the following income statement.***

1. Can you pick out four items that are over the industry average?

2. Is the owner intelligently buying merchandise for resale?

3. What does 1% represent in dollars?

4. How much more money would the owner have if the telephone bill could be reduced to the industry average?

5. Even though the gross profit percentage is larger than the industry average, the net profit is smaller. Why?

ABC Emporium
Income Statement
Date

				%	% Ind Ave
Sales (less discounts and allowances)			$ 700,000	100	100
Cost of Goods Sold			500,000	71.4	72.4
Gross Profit			200,000	28.6	27.6
Expenses					
Drawings (owners)	42,000	6.0	6.0		
Wages	58,100	8.3	10.0		
Delivery	7,000	1.0	1.4		
Bad Debt	2,100	.3	.7		
Telephone	9,100	1.3	.4		
Depreciation	4,200	.6	1.0		
Insurance	6,300	.9	.7		
Taxes (local)	7,700	1.1	1.0		

(continues on next page)

(continued)

Interest	15,400	2.2	1.0
Advertising	23,800	3.4	1.5
Miscellaneous	2,100	.3	.5
Total	177,800	25.4	24.2

Net Profit (before federal taxes)	22,200	3.2	3.4

The answers are in Appendix D.

BARTERING

What once was used only rarely is now becoming organized and growing. Bartering today is not just an easy trade between friends and relatives, it now involves an annual $5 billion exchange of services or goods between 400 trade associations nationwide.

Businesses swap everything from plumbing services for advertising to computers for vacations. More businesses are discovering that when a cash crunch comes, bartering is an answer that lets them get what they want. It also is a good way to attract new customers in a competitive market.

JOINING AN EXCHANGE

The most effective way to barter is to join one of the many exchanges that trade nationwide. These exchanges use large computer databases to match and expedite member requests.

Some exchanges have reciprocal privileges with other exchanges, so you are not limited to just one exchange. It works like this. The exchange sets up a system of trade "dollars" that replaces the use of cash. After you establish an account you can purchase goods or services from other members, who can "buy" from you. The exchange tracks all of this and you can build up the "dollars" and buy what you need regardless of who bought

There is usually a one-time membership fee of several hundred dollars and a commission charge of 10% or more for each transaction. The commission is paid by the buyer, seller or both, depending on the exchange policy. Exchanges usually publish newsletters and maintain a 24-hour telephone service. You can usually determine how much you want to sell and where you want to market your goods and services so that you don't interfere with your cash sales.

You are not forgotten by Uncle Sam: The exchanges process earnings records to the IRS. The IRS considers each sale a cash transaction and reportable as income. Likewise, all barter "purchases" for business purposes can be deducted from gross income.

Exchanges can help small businesses get what they need, but use them with caution:

- ▶ Exchanges are not completely regulated by the government. Investigate several and request member lists for verification. Be sure you fit the exchange's market.

- ▶ If you can't use the goods or service, or can't handle the extra business that may be created, don't barter for barter's sake.

- ▶ Have a goal; for example, to use up all your production capacity, to enter new markets, to get rid of excess inventory.

- ▶ Be flexible. Your current suppliers may not belong to the exchange, so you will need to do business with others.

- ▶ Don't forget to negotiate. Even barter prices are negotiable, which may be why the goods are there to begin with.

- ▶ Don't neglect your cash business as you build up "barter points." You still must replace sold merchandise, which presumably can't be obtained with barter credits.

REVIEW

▶ Expenses are a normal part of doing business

▶ Expenses can and should be controlled so you will know what you are getting for them

▶ Begin your expense examination by analyzing sales

▶ Next, take a look at cost of goods sold; see if it has increased or decreased and if so, try to find out why

▶ Fixed expenses should not vary with any increase or decrease in sales

▶ Variable expenses change with your sales volume

▶ When you think you have cut expenses to the bone, examine the eight major areas of your business to increase your return on expenses

▶ Bartering may be a way to increase your business by allowing you to get into different markets and attract customers that don't trade with you now

ASK YOURSELF

► Describe the special happenings such as weather, competitor's marketing, suppliers increasing prices or affecting delivery, etc., that might have an effect on your sales.

► What unusual charges, spoilage, theft, etc., could increase your cost of goods sold?

► Will I be sure my variable expenses are in line with or better than the industry's?

► Compare your gross profit with your net profit.

► Explain your credit policy.

► What criteria will you use to determine when to add an employee?

► Discuss the importance of lifecycle costs when considering new equipment.

CHAPTER TEN

ASSET MANAGEMENT

MANAGING THE CASH ACCOUNT

Current assets—cash, accounts receivable and inventory—are important to any business, because they pay the bills for raw materials, wages, rent and other expenses. Without sufficient current assets, a business could not survive. The cash account contains all the "real" money the business has. Accounts receivable presumably will be paid, but as of the day the balance sheet is dated, they haven't been. The inventory may or may not be sold for the amount shown on the balance sheet—only time will tell. (For service businesses, inventory is probably not a factor.)

The goal is to find that magic point between cash collections and cash expenditures. Cash tied up in inventory or receivables cannot be counted on to pay your bills. So when you restock, be careful that you leave enough cash to pay your bills.

There are ways to shorten collection periods. Of course, your suppliers will use them on you to collect any money you owe them. These methods include:

- Review receivables often, at least once a month
- Create discount terms that make it profitable for customers to pay promptly, but watch out that this "cost" doesn't become a penalty
- Monitor each customer's payment trends
- Establish minimum order and invoice amounts for credit sales and set service fees for any credit order less than the minimum
- Be sure your policies are in writing and are consistently enforced
- Settle any disputes quickly
- Contact late payers by telephone first
- Recognize that large corporations and government offices nearly always pay late
- Maintain an accounts receivable aging schedule to help identify late payers
- Send the bill the same day the merchandise was sent or picked up

Just as you want to shorten collection periods from your customers, you want to lengthen cash payouts to your creditors. This means delaying payments as long as possible while taking advantage of significant discounts and not jeopardizing your vendors and suppliers.

▶ Determine if the discount is as good as what you can earn on the money you would have to pay if you waited the full term (usually 30 days).

▶ When considering volume buys because of a discount, look at cash outflow, storage space, insurance, spoilage, theft and possible increased tax.

▶ Limit the number of suppliers, especially of the same item. Look for the fastest supplier, other things being equal, which can cut inventory carrying costs.

▶ Try to get a discount for volume over time rather than each shipment. If a supplier gets all your business, they may be receptive.

▶ Don't automatically pay sales tax. Check to see if items for resale are exempt.

▶ Find a bank that pays interest on checking accounts. If you can't get one, see if an automatic transfer of funds from savings to checking can be arranged.

▶ Deposit all receipts daily.

▶ If you believe you will be short of cash, call your creditors and try to get an extension or make a partial payment now and the rest later without penalty.

▶ Assume all payment deadlines are negotiable.

▶ Don't abuse your suppliers' good faith. Be honest with them in the good times and you will stand a better chance of being helped during the lean times.

MANAGING RECEIVABLES POLICY

If you are thinking about increasing sales by extending more credit or loosening credit policy, you should ask these questions: If sales rise, will expenses (labor, material, cost of financing or carrying the extra credit and bad debts) also increase and by how much? Will it be worth the expense to ease the restrictions on granting credit as a means to gain higher sales?

Things that must be considered are:

- ▶ Projected additional sales
- ▶ Discounts for early payment (what percent; for example, 2% if paid within 10 days)
- ▶ Increase in late payments (what percent of sales and for what length of time)
- ▶ Increase in inventory (and all associated costs)
- ▶ Where to finance (equity or debt)
- ▶ Is there excess manufacturing capacity (and trained operators)
- ▶ Opportunity costs (the loss of other areas to use debt or equity)
- ▶ Increase in bad debts (at what percent of sales)

The projected analysis of credit policy on an accounts receivable profit chart has blank spaces to fill in with your data. It provides a comparison of the old and new policies, parentheses for percentage comparisons and a column for dollar difference comparisons. The questionnaire that follows will help you think through all the things you should consider before changing your credit policy. The use of these charts may seem time consuming, but they help you make good decisions and take calculated risks in developing your business. Try this analysis with your company's data.

Projected

Analysis of Credit Policy
on Accounts Receivable Profit
End of year

	%	Projected Income Old Policy	Effect of Policy Change	Projected Income New Policy	%
Sales	(100)	_____	_____	_____	( )
Cost of Goods Sold	( )	_____	_____	_____	( )
Gross Profit Before Discounts	( )	_____	_____	_____	( )
Minus Discounts	( )	_____	_____	_____	( )
Gross Profit	( )	_____	_____	_____	( )
Operating Expenses	( )	_____	_____	_____	( )
Profit Before Credit Costs and Taxes	( )	_____	_____	_____	( )
Credit Operation Expenses	( )	_____	_____	_____	( )
Cost of Carrying Receivables	( )	_____	_____	_____	( )
Bad Debt Losses	( )	_____	_____	_____	( )
Profit Before Taxes	( )	_____	_____	_____	( )
Taxes (@)	( )	_____	_____	_____	( )
Net Income	( )	_____	_____	_____	( )

Things I must consider:

Projected sales $_____

Discounts $_____

Increase in late payments _____%

Increase in inventory $_____

(continues on next page)

Where to finance Debt? Equity?

Is there excess manufacturing
or other required capacity? Yes No

Any lost opportunity costs? Have they been evaluated?

Results _____

_____

_____

_____

Will there be an increase in bad debts? Yes No

If yes, by how much? $_____

What percent increase? _____%

Will credit operation expenses rise or fall? Yes No

By how much? $_____ _____%

Will cost of carrying receivables rise? Yes No

By how much? $_____ _____%

Analysis: _____

_____

_____

_____

INVENTORY MANAGEMENT

Inventory management is critical to your firm's success. Understanding carrying costs, ordering costs of inventory, liquidating excess inventory and recognizing danger signs are all elements of inventory management.

Carrying costs include the cost of money that can't be used for something else, storage and handling costs, insurance, depreciation, taxes, spoilage and theft. These costs generally rise or fall with the amount of inventory carried. The amount of inventory carried is the annual sales in units divided by the number of orders placed per year, divided by two. (The quantity ordered should be based on the economic order quantity.)

$$\frac{\text{Sales in units / number of orders}}{2}$$

(Note: If your store carries multiple units, this calculation should be done for each unit.)

For example: Sales + 20,000 units; number of orders = 5

$$\frac{20,000 / 5}{2} =$$ 20,000 units is the average inventory, which ranges from 40,000 to 0 or whatever your reorder point turns out to be. Multiplying this by the cost per unit gives the amount of inventory value ($5 per unit cost × 20,000 = $100,000).

To determine total carrying costs you need these figures:

Cost of money (percent to borrow or, if equity is used, the net profit percentage): For this problem assume the cost of money is 10%.

Cost to carry the inventory: Percent of the cost of money × the average inventory, or .10 × $100,000 = $10,000.

Storage costs (space, bins, racks, utilities, security, handling labor): For this problem assume storage costs are $4,000.

Insurance costs: For this problem assume insurance costs are $200.

Spoilage/theft costs: For this problem assume spoilage/theft costs are $100.

The total cost of carrying the $100,000 average inventory is $10,000 + $4,000 + $200 + $100 = $14,300. The percentage cost of carrying the inventory is

$$\frac{\$14,300}{\$100,000} = 14.3\%.$$

If the percentage carrying cost is known, you can multiply it times the cost per unit times the average inventory in units. $.143 \times \$5 \times 20,000 = \$14,300$ inventory carrying costs.

ORDERING COSTS

Ordering costs, unlike carrying costs, are generally fixed costs. These costs consist of:

Cost to place an order (labor, telephone, forms, postage): Assume for this problem the cost is $25.

Cost to receive an order (labor, handling, storage, breakage, stocking, shipping, payment forms, postage): Assume for this problem the cost is $50.

Total ordering costs = $75 × the number of orders per year. Assuming the number of orders placed is five, the total costs are $375. The total inventory costs are therefore: total ordering costs + total carrying costs or $375 + $14,300 = $14,675.

DANGER SIGNS

Stocking items unnecessarily for any length of time will drain your resources, because your capital could go to other areas such as paying debts. This drain may cause more debt because the interest and carrying charges can run as high as 25% of the total inventory.

Signals to watch for:

▶ Inventories climbing faster than sales

▶ A noticeable shift of inventory mix

▶ Disparities between stock and accounting records

- ▶ Write-offs for obsolete materials are increasing
- ▶ Back orders and lead times are increasing as well as customer complaints
- ▶ Turnover rates are below average for the industry
- ▶ Material costs are rising faster than overall product costs

---

Your Turn

This inventory exercise will help you see if you understand the chapter.

Item	Item amount, cost or percent
Annual sales in units	150,000
Number of orders placed per year	20
Cost per unit	$10
Cost of money	8.0%
Storage costs	$3,000
Insurance costs	$100
Spoilage and theft	$100
Cost to place an order	$20
Cost to receive the order	$35

What is the total inventory cost?

Answer is in Appendix D.

REDUCING OBSOLETE INVENTORY

Sometimes you may need to get rid of obsolete inventory. Rather than throw it out, here are some ideas that may help you make the best of it.

1. *Hold a sale*

   You will probably get a better price from regular customers than from unloading the items on the market in general.

2. *Return it*

   It may be possible that the original supplier will take back part of the order. You may not get the full amount or you may only get credit on the next order, but at least you got something.

3. *Convert it*

   Sometimes it is possible to use the excess inventory to make up other items with another store's obsolete items to make a more attractive offer.

4. *Trade it*

   Several firms offer services for liquidating inventory.

5. *Add on to it*

   Use obsolete inventory as free add-ons for those purchasing a certain amount of other goods or services.

6. *Donate it*

   You may find a charity that can use the items. The donation can be a public relations gesture and may even be a tax deduction.

LEASING

Leasing may be an alternative for acquiring the use of fixed assets. All types of equipment leasing, from motor vehicles to computers and from production equipment to office furniture, have become more attractive.

A lease is a long-term agreement to rent equipment, land, buildings or any other asset in return for most of the benefits of ownership, without putting down a large amount of cash and securing a long-term loan. Leasing is also called "off balance sheet" financing, since the leased assets do not appear on the balance sheet as they would if they were owned.

The three major kinds of leases are financial, operating and sale and lease-back. A financial lease, usually written for a term not to exceed the economic life of the equipment, is the most common. The terms usually include periodic payments, a non-cancellation clause and agreements that ownership of the equipment usually reverts to the lessor and the lessee will maintain the equipment.

The operating lease is used for computer and other equipment that is maintained by the leasing company. The agreement can usually be terminated as specified by the agreement.

The sale and lease-back arrangement is like the financial lease except that the owner of an asset sells it and at the same time leases it back. This arrangement is usually used to free up money to use elsewhere.

Advantages of leasing include:

- ► Having the use of an asset without putting down a lot of money
- ► Carries fewer financial restrictions than a loan might
- ► Spreads payments over time, usually longer than a loan would permit
- ► A true lease arrangement permits some tax benefits, because the payments count as an expense deduction
- ► The leasing firm understands the equipment they lease, which can be of enormous help

The disadvantages of leasing include:

- ► Leasing may cost more
- ► You lose certain tax advantages if you have enough tax liability to make it worthwhile
- ► The normal lease is long-term and usually cannot be canceled

As with any financial arrangement, be cautious. Investigate the lessor's reputation and financial condition. Because a lease is a long-term legal arrangement, be fully informed: Evaluate lease costs vs. loan costs, using net present value analysis to determine your best option. An accountant, bank or other loan institution can help with this. Finally, be sure that you need the equipment and the contract is what you want—then negotiate for the best agreement you can get.

ASK YOURSELF

► Why are current assets important?

► Describe the three important items to consider when changing your credit policy.

► How do you determine the turnover of accounts receivable?

► What are accounts receivable?

► Explain why you should only consider variable expenses in determining the effect of a new credit policy to increase sales.

► What costs are associated with placing an order?

► How do you determine inventory value?

► Discuss the relationship between the cost of money and the cost of borrowing the money.

► How do storage costs affect your business?

HOW TO CONTROL
YOUR BUSINESS

HOW TO FORECAST FINANCES

Of the several ways to control your business, some of the better ones involve financial analysis. Control means not just trying to meet a standard or the industry average. It means helping you to plan ahead—for example, by forecasting how much money it will take to expand your present sales or prepare for a big promotional sale to introduce a new product line.

Control works two ways. First, it helps you do better what you are now doing. Second, it helps you prepare for expansion or change without being caught short of cash because you forgot an expense or did not have a plan to keep things in balance. Five control techniques that can help shape your business are trend analysis, debt coverage ratio, accounts receivable aging schedule, credit collection tips and managing working capital.

TREND ANALYSIS

The data gathering form (p. 106), comparison chart (p. 107) and ratio and percentage analysis will aid you in doing a trend analysis, which is simply a method of monitoring month-to-month and year-to-year ratios and expenses. Let's suppose that our two companies have been in business for three years. We will now compare their progress by doing a trend analysis.

Four charts have been designed to help you do this. The first tracks your month-to-month ratios, the second tracks your year-to-year ratios. The third monitors month-to-month expenses and the fourth monitors year-to-year expenses. Make a copy of each monthly chart at the beginning of your business year, and label each column by the name of the month. Next, record the month ending ratios or expenses in the proper column, which builds a monthly trend. Recording each year end ratio and expense on each yearly chart will build a yearly trend. Use the last column to list your goal or industry averages for each ratio. By doing this you will have a history of how well you are doing. Keep these records handy for your review; analysis will help you plan future actions.

Two other charts show how you can use trends to help you understand your business. The ratio comparison chart provides a three-year look at the Pumping Iron Fitness Center and the Hi-Tech Merchandise Company. We will assume that the owners want to match or come close to the industry averages.

Remember that you should think about selecting your own percentages if the industry averages are unavailable owing to the type or age of your business, its location or business cycle. The percentages used on the following charts are fictional and used to make an analytical conclusion.

Pumping Iron Fitness Center

RATIO COMPARISON

THREE YEARS

Ratio	1st Year	2nd Year	3rd Year	Industry Average
Current Assets / Current Liabilities	1.4%	1.8 T	2.1 T	2.1 T
Sales / Working Capital	22.7 T	12.2 T	9.5 T	8.7 T
Total Debt / Net Sales	10.3 T	12.6 T	7.1 T	60.0%
EBIT / Net Sales	41.2%	32.7%	32.2%	39.5%
Net Profit / Net Sales	31.2%	24.0%	25.2%	30.1%
Net Profit / Net Worth	3.4 T	2.7 T	2.7 T	40.2 T
Net Profit / Total Assets	29.8%	26.4%	33.8%	28.1%
Accounts Receivable × 365 / Credit Sales	6.0 D	11.0 D	13.0 D	23.0 D
Cost of Goods Sold / Average Inventory*	2.1 T	2.4 T	2.1 T	N/A
Fixed Assets / Net Worth	9.8 T	8.2 T	5.9 T	30.0%
Net Sales / Total Assets	95.5%	1.1 T	1.3 T	2.2 T
Net Sales / Fixed Assets	1.1 T	1.4 T	1.8 T	5.5 T

T = Times; D = Average number of days it takes to collect credit sales

$$\text{*Average Inventory} = \frac{\text{beginning inventory} + \text{ending inventory}}{2}$$

$$\text{1st year} = \frac{0 + \$14,200}{2} = 7,100$$

$$\text{2nd year} = \frac{\$14,200 + \$12,000}{2} = \$13,100$$

$$\text{3rd year} = \frac{\$12,000 + \$7,000}{2} = 9,500$$

Pumping Iron Fitness Center

EXPENSE COMPARISON

THREE YEARS

Expense Item	1st Year		2nd Year		3rd Year		Industry Average
	Dollar Amount	%	Dollar Amount	%	Dollar Amount	%	%
Net Sales	300,000	100	330,000	100	390,000	100	100
Credit Sales	(42,600	14.2	92,500	28	123,500	31.7)	
Cost of Sales (Equipment)	30,000	10.0	32,000	9.7	20,000	5.2	11.5
Gross Profit (Service)	(225,000	75.0	250,000	75.8	300,000	77.0)	
Gross Profit (Equipment)	(75,000	25.0	80,000	24.2	90,000	23.0)	
Total Gross Profit	270,000	90.0	298,000	90.3	370,000	94.8	88.5
Expenses:							
Drawings (Owner)	40,000	13.3	40,000	12.1	60,000	15.4	N/A
Salaries	42,100	14.0	75,000	22.7	100,000	25.6	23.5

Expense Item	1st Year		2nd Year		3rd Year		Industry Average
	Dollar Amount	%	Dollar Amount	%	Dollar Amount	%	%
Vacation/Sick	1,130	.4	1,200	.4	4,200	1.0	
Health Insurance	3,900	1.3	4,140	1.3	6,140	1.6	
Unemployment Insurance	760	.3	960	.3	2,000	.5	6.6
Social Security/ Workers Compensation	700	.2	900	.3	1,500	.4	
Life Insurance	1,800	.6	1,600	.5	1,800	.5	
Consumable Supplies	1,200	.4	1,000	.3	2,000	.5	1.0
Repairs and Maintenance	1,000	.4	800	.2	1,800	.5	2.7
Advertising	4,800	1.5	5,800	1.7	8,800	2.3	1.6
Professional Expenses	1,800	.6	1,800	.5	1,800	.5	0
Mortgage Principal	2,534	.8	2,784	.8	3,060	.8	1.0
Loan Principal	11,346	3.8	12,536	3.8	13,848	3.5	2.0
Telephone	3,500	1.2	3,100	.9	4,000	1.0	3.8
Utilities	3,600	1.2	3,600	1.1	4,200	1.0	2.6
Business Insurance	3,000	1.0	3,000	1.0	4,000	1.0	1.6
Taxes	4,560	1.5	4,560	1.4	4,560	1.2	2.5
Interest	25,483	8.5	24,041	7.3	22,447	5.8	5.5
Depreciation	21,960	7.3	21,960	6.6	21,960	5.6	5.5
Miscellaneous	1,200	.4	2,000	.6	3,500	.9	0
Total Expenses	176,373	58.8	210,781	64.0	271,615	69.6	59.9*
Net Profit	93,627	31.2	82,219	26.3	98,385	25.2	28.6

( ) = Information figures
0 = Not listed
% Increase in sales = percent increase in sales each year
Gross profit service and gross profit equipment = Sales
Sales minus cost of sales equipment = Total gross profit
*+5.1% = Loans, professional expenses, miscellaneous, etc., included.

Pumping Iron Fitness Center

BALANCE SHEET COMPARISON

THREE YEARS

	1st Year		2nd Year		3rd Year		Industry Average
ASSETS	Dollar Amount	%	Dollar Amount	%	Dollar Amount	%	%
Cash	30,000	9.6	40,000	13.7	56,000	19.2	8.9
Accounts Receivable	5,000	1.6	10,000	3.3	14,000	4.8	15.3
Inventory	14,200	4.5	12,000	4.0	7,000	2 5	4 2
Other							2.8
Total C/A	49,200	15.6	62,000	20.7	77,000	26.5	31.2
Building	106,400	33.9	91,000	30.3	75,000	25.7	68.8
Equipment/Fixtures	158,500	50.5	147,000	49.0	139,000	47.8	
Total Fixed Assets	264,900	84.4	238,000	79.3	214,000	73.5	68.8
Total Assets	314,100	100	300,000	100	291,000	100	100.0
LIABILITIES							
Accounts Payable	20,000	6.4	21,000	7.0	11,000	3.8	5.2
Accruals	16,000	5.1	14,000	4.7	25,000	8.6	5.1
Notes Payable							10.3
Current Tax							.9
Other							9.8
Total C/L	36,000	15.3	35,000	11.7	36,000	12.4	31.3
LONG-TERM DEBT							
10 Year Note	173,654	55.3	161,118	53.7	147,270	50.6	26.8
Mortgage	77,466	24.7	74,682	24.9	71,622	24.6	
Other							3.6
Deferred Tax							.7
ASSETS	Dollar Amount	%	Dollar Amount	%	Dollar Amount	%	%
Total Long-Term Debt	251,120	79.9	235,800	78.6	218,892	75.2	31.1
NET WORTH	26,980	8.6	29,200	9.7	36,108	12.4	37.6
Total Liabilities/Net Worth	314,100	100	300,000	100	291,000	100	100.0

In analyzing expenses, balances and ratios to spot trends, you should question each figure to determine if it corresponds to what you expect. Ask yourself if it is reasonable for the situation (business age, industry, competition, location or external factors such as weather). Question whether the ratio or percent makes sense, ask why it is good, how could it be better, if it becomes better will something else suffer. This analysis will examine trends over three years to determine if the company is making reasonable progress, where its strengths and weaknesses are and what should be done in the future.

PUMPING IRON FITNESS CENTER TREND ANALYSIS (RATIOS)

Liquidity: The Pumping Iron Fitness Center is moving in the right direction: The current asset to current liability ratio and the turnover of working capital to sales ratio are both good. However, total debt is still too large compared to net worth, but the trend shows that the firm is slowly easing out of debt.

Profitability: If we compare the EBIT and net profit to sales ratios, we find that after a roaring start, they dropped. Now the ratios are slightly low but holding. This ratio will increase with growth; the trend looks good.

Profit to net worth is low, which is not a good situation, but this ratio should get better as debt is reduced and net worth increases. Net profit should be higher than net worth and will be as the owners pay for the business.

The return on assets ratio (net profit/total assets) indicates that the business is very good at getting a high return on assets. High returns may be owing to higher margins, because these assets will support more sales. These margins may not hold up if strong competition comes in, but now the use of assets is good.

Efficiency: Accounts receivable started off well, but as credit sales increased, later payments also increased. However, this company is well within the standard and probably could loosen up credit still more if it would attract more sales. The company seems to attract higher-income customers, who like to pay as they go.

Fixed assets as a part of net worth is slowly coming in line, but there are still too few sales for the amount of assets. Net sales to total and fixed assets still does not meet industry standards, especially for fixed assets, but the trend is improving.

Summary: If more paid sales cannot be obtained, the owner should investigate reducing the building and equipment—perhaps by leasing a part of the building and selling some equipment. If a lap pool, sauna or hot tub is involved, this may be difficult. Overall, the business is behaving like a start-up that was financed by long-term debt. It needs more sales and fewer assets.

EXPENSES ANALYSIS

Look at the top of the income statement and note the sales over the three-year period. Each year sales increased by 9% and 15%, but profits first decreased by 18% then increased by 19%. Since gross profit increased slightly, the decrease had to come from increased expenses, which was principally wages and benefits, although some first-year expenses may have been paid in the second year.

The cost of sales is beating the standard, and membership trends shown by gross profit service are increasing by 10% and 17%. If this trend continues, the sales to asset ratio will improve. Total gross sales have increased each year because the company is carrying less inventory, thus lowering the cost of sales figure.

The owner's drawings is on target, although the standard is not available. The salaries and benefits of the help are within bounds after the first year, which was apparently necessary to sustain the sales.

Supplies and repair are below standards, which may be because the company is new and the assets (such as the workout equipment) were underutilized. Advertising rose during the third year and exceeded the standard. The increase in sales helped to offset the advertising increase.

Debt (loan/mortgage) and interest and depreciation continue to be high, probably because the business is still new. So, except that sales are low, not much else is out of line. Remember that this analysis compares a new business to the averages of all reporting businesses in the industry or regional businesses that started in the last five years and have nearly the same sales as your business. If you can get averages closer to your trading area, your analysis will have more meaning. Maybe this can be done through your trade association.

ANALYSIS FROM THE BALANCE SHEET

Look first at the general categories: current assets, fixed assets, current liabilities, long-term debt and net worth. Next look at the subcategories. Current asset trends are below industry averages, so let's see what subcategories are the lowest. Certainly cash is not. Accounts receivables is low but growing, and inventory is about right. These figures indicate that more credit could be extended.

The "other" account shown by the averages is possibly a certificate of deposit or other savings, which is normal for an older business. If this 2.8% is subtracted, the industry average almost will be met.

The fixed assets trend is heading in the right direction. In about two years it will reach the standard and go below it unless new equipment is bought, the building is fixed up or other measures are taken to increase fixed asset values.

Current liabilities are low. It appears that most of the industry finances with short-term loans and notes rather than long-term debt and procurement of fixed assets. The long-term debt trend seems to confirm this. As a general rule, long-term debt is preferred to short-term financing.

As expected for a new start, net worth is low, but this is explained by the high debt.

Summary: This business needs to see if it can increase sales or reduce fixed assets, unless it expects sales to continue to grow. Possibilities for the sale or other use of the fixed assets include renting a part of the building, selling the equipment and leasing part of it back and mounting a membership campaign to increase revenue.

Hi-Tech Merchandise Company

RATIO COMPARISON

THREE YEARS

Ratio	1st Year	2nd Year	3rd Year	Industry Average
$\dfrac{\text{Current Assets}}{\text{Current Liabilities}}$	1.4 T	1.7 T	1.6 T	1.8 T
$\dfrac{\text{Sales}}{\text{Working Capital}}$	5.9 T	4.6 T	5.3 T	8.9 T
$\dfrac{\text{Total Debt}}{\text{Net Worth}}$	2.6 T	2.0 T	2.3 T	1.8 T
$\dfrac{\text{EBIT}}{\text{Net Sales}}$	5.2 %	3.5%	6.0%	3.8%
$\dfrac{\text{Net Profit}}{\text{Net Sales}}$	2.5%	1.0%	3.6%	2.9%
$\dfrac{\text{Net Profit}}{\text{Net Worth}}$	10.3%	3.8%	16.6%	30.1%
$\dfrac{\text{Net Profit}}{\text{Total Assets}}$	3.0%	1.3%	5.0%	15.1%
$\dfrac{\text{Accounts Receivable} \times 365}{\text{Credit Sales}}$	88.0 D	86.6 D	76.3 D	39 D
$\dfrac{\text{Cost of Goods Sold}}{\text{Average Inventory*}}$	5.6 T	3.1 T	3.2 T	11.8 T
$\dfrac{\text{Fixed Assets}}{\text{Net Worth}}$	1.2 T	94.0%	1.0 T	30.0 %
$\dfrac{\text{Net Sales}}{\text{Total Assets}}$	1.2 T	1.3 T	1.4 T	4.4 T
$\dfrac{\text{Net Sales}}{\text{Fixed Assets}}$	3.4 T	4.0 T	3.2 T	11.6 T

T = Times; D = Average number of days it takes to collect credit sales

$$\text{*Average Inventory} = \frac{\text{beginning inventory} + \text{ending inventory}}{2}$$

$$\text{1st year} = \frac{0 + \$200{,}000}{2} = \$100{,}000$$

$$\text{2nd year} = \frac{\$200{,}000 + \$192{,}000}{2} = \$196{,}000$$

$$\text{3rd year} = \frac{\$192{,}000 + \$165{,}000}{2} = \$178{,}500$$

Hi-Tech Merchandise Company

EXPENSE COMPARISON

THREE YEARS

Expense Item	1st Year		2nd Year		3rd Year		Industry Average
	Dollar Amount	%	Dollar Amount	%	Dollar Amount	%	%
Net Sales	766,990	100	800,000	100	789,000	100	100
Credit Sales	(575,000	75	560,000	70	536,520	69)	
Cost of Goods Sold	560,000	73	600,000	75	568,080	72	70.9
Gross Profit	206,990	27	200,000	25	220,920	28	29.1
Expenses:							
Drawings (Owner)	14,000	1.8	20,000	2.5	30,000	3.8	4.7
Salaries	65,000	8.5	65,000	8.1	52,000	6.6	6.0
Benefits/Social Security	7,790	1.0	8,450	1.1	7,000	.9	1.0
Delivery	12,200	1.6	14,000	1.8	20,000	2.5	1.5
Bad Debt	4,000	.6	2,000	.2	500		.4
Professional Expenses	2,000	.2	2,000	.2	2,000	.3	.5
Telephone	2,000	.2	1,890	.2	1,700	.2	.6

Expense Item	1st Year		2nd Year		3rd Year		Industry Average
	Dollar Amount	%	Dollar Amount	%	Dollar Amount	%	%
Depreciation	24,000	3.1	24,000	3.0	24,000	3.0	1.4
Repairs and Consumables	2,200	.3	2,200	.3	3,000	.4	.3
Life Insurance	1,800	.2	1,500	.2	750	——	.1
Utilities	3,000	.4	3,000	.4	3,000	.4	.9
Business Insurance	7,000	.9	7,000	.9	4,500	.6	.8
Taxes	8,000	1.1	8,000	1.0	8,000	1.0	1.2
Interest	12,447	1.6	12,000	1.5	11,500	1.5	.3
Loan Principal	7,875	1.1	8,122	1.1	8,372	1.1	1.5
Mortgage Principal	2,477	.3	2,677	.3	2,927	.4	1.9
Advertising	5,000	.7	5,000	.6	8,700	1.2	2.8
Miscellaneous	7,000	.9	5,000	.6	3,500	.5	.7
Total Expenses	187,789	24.5	191,839	24.0	191,449	24.4	26.1
Net Profit	19,201	2.5	8,161	1.0	29,471	3.6	2.5

( ) = Information figures

% Increase in sales = percent increase in sales each year

Hi-Tech Merchandise Company

BALANCE SHEET COMPARISON

THREE YEARS

	1st Year		2nd Year		3rd Year		Industry Average
	Dollar Amount	%	Dollar Amount	%	Dollar Amount	%	%
ASSETS							
Cash	52,000	7.8	50,000	7.9	55,000	9.6	8.1
Accounts Receivable	185,000	28.0	190,000	30.1	165,000	28.8	31.2
Inventory	200,000	30.2	192,000	30.3	175,000	30.6	34.3
Other							2.0
Total C/A	437,000	66.0	432,000	68.3	395,000	69.0	75.6
Building	150,000	22.7	130,000	20.5	110,000	19.2	⎫ 24.2
Equipment/Fixtures	75,000	11.3	71,000	11.2	67,000	11.7	⎭
Total F/A	225,000	34.0	201,000	31.7	177,000	30.9	24.4
Total Assets	662,000	100	633,000	100	572,000	100	100.0
LIABILITIES							
Accounts Payable	205,000	31.0	150,000	23.7	160,000	28.0	20.4
Accruals	46,000	6.9	56,000	8.9	42,000	7.3	16.3
Notes Payable	58,000	8.8	51,000	8.0	43,000	7.5	19.1
Total C/L	309,000	46.7	257,000	40.6	245,000	42.8	55.8
LONG-TERM DEBT							
8 Year Note	63,000	9.5	60,000	9.5	56,000	9.8	⎫ 18.7
Mortgage	104,300	15.8	102,000	16.1	100,000	17.5	⎭
Total Long-Term Debt	167,300	25.3	162,000	25.6	156,000	27.3	18.7
NET WORTH	185,700	28.0	214,000	33.8	171,000	29.9	25.5
Total Liabilities/Net worth	662,000	100	633,000	100	572,000	100	100.0

HI-TECH MERCHANDISE COMPANY
TREND ANALYSIS (RATIO)

Liquidity: The trend shows that the Hi-Tech Merchandise Company is doing well and moving in the right direction. The company still has not achieved the standard, which is confirmed by the working capital turnover ratio. Although sales were higher in the second year, cost of goods sold also was higher, probably because of last-minute ordering and late payments. As a whole, current assets are fine and debt reduction is going slowly but in the right direction.

Profitability: Looking at EBIT and net profit to sales indicates that the profit margin meets the industry standard, so the pricing structure is good. However, the company could use more cash and inventory planning.

Net profit to net worth is another indication of profitability. During the first year of operation, this figure was good, the second year it was worse, the third year it improved again, but it is still short of where it should be. Net worth percents show that it is above the standard. Therefore, profit dollars need to be increased through sales, because margins and total expenses are good. Note that net profit grew in the third year but net worth did not, because current assets fell much more than current liabilities. The return on assets ratio jumped down and up and is still too low, which reveals that the assets will support more sales or fewer assets will provide the same profits.

Efficiency: Accounts receivable is improving but still weak, which is one reason the business lacks cash to pay suppliers. This situation can be helped with more cash sales, faster collections or less inventory, but less inventory may lead to less business if customers have to wait.

Fixed assets are too great a part of new worth, but this is to be expected from a new business. Net sales to total assets and to fixed assets show that assets can support a lot more sales. If sales don't improve, the owners should consider reducing both current and fixed assets such as inventory, building and equipment. A reduction in fixed assets may be realized with a sell and lease-back arrangement or using part of the building for something else.

Summary: This trend analysis shows that inventory and net worth could improve with more sales and less debt. The need for assets needs to be re-evaluated.

A trend analysis for expenses can be determined by examining the income statement and balance sheet, which have been percentaged (called common sizing). Sales increased about 4% in the second year, then declined about 1.4% the third year. This fluctuation may be the nature of the business, but sales need to grow steadily.

The cost of goods sold jumped 2% the second year, which is 5% over standard. Cost of goods sold in the third year is heading in the right direction but still needs a little work. Perhaps the business lacks cash to pay early for the discounts that the rest of the industry apparently gets. The total expenses are lower than the standard, which is a good sign.

Owner's drawings are lower than average. Salaries are higher than average, but they come in line in the third year. Benefits are about on target.

Delivery costs are higher than average. This expense should be checked to see if both figures (the industry average and Hi-Tech) include the same items (insurance, taxes, salaries, maintenance, etc.). The owner is holding down bad debt, probably by operating conservatively, which was noted in the average days collection ratio. Professional and telephone expenses are lower than the standard, and as might be expected, depreciation is quite large. These depreciated assets can support more sales.

Repair/maintenance and life insurance costs are average, while the cost of utilities is well below average. Perhaps the "averages" contain more utilities such as water, gas and electricity than the Hi-Tech account does.

Insurance, taxes and the loan principal are also within range of industry standards, but the interest expense is high as it would be with a new start financed largely by debt. The mortgage principal is low, perhaps because it is paid over a longer period of time than that of the industry average. Advertising is low, and maybe it should be increased if it would increase sales. Miscellaneous is in line with the average.

Summary: This trend analysis matches very closely with what we learned from the ratio trend analysis. Using more advertising to increase sales is a possibility, and looking sharply at the delivery charge is a must. Keeping the accounts that are average or lower than the average is also important. Assets, especially fixed assets, should be reduced if sales do not improve.

Now let's see if the balance sheet analysis confirms the other trend analysis or reveals something new. Current assets comprise 54.8% compared to the standard of 75.6%. Fixed assets are somewhat the reverse, 45.2% for Hi-Tech to 24.4% for the average. The fact that fixed assets are a large part of total assets and net worth goes along with the other trends. The current asset accounts are good: high in cash and low in receivables and inventory, but the owners could be too conservative in extending credit and thus are missing some sales (remember the bad debt account and fast collection period). More inventory might help sales, but since inventory turnover is quite low this does not seem to be an answer unless the wrong inventory is being carried.

The liabilities trend reveals that current liabilities are lower than the standard, but the accounts payable account is higher than the standard. These figures indicate that the owners are missing trade payments, losing some discounts (as previously thought) and running the risk of alienating some suppliers. It also appears that the industry uses more short-term loans than long-term debt, which is confirmed by comparing the long-term debt percentages.

Net worth is well below the standard but would rise dramatically if trade payables were reduced substantially and the cash account stayed the same. This reduction would also help the cost of goods sold percentage as discounts are taken. Of course, reduction of debt would also help the business, and this will probably happen over time.

Summary: The Hi-Tech Merchandise Company should use some of its cash and profits to pay its bills, reduce delivery costs to gain funds and make an effort to increase sales by increasing advertising or extending more credit. If these tactics don't work, Hi-Tech should then consider reducing its assets, both fixed and current, to a level that matches the level of sales the company can obtain.

Sales increased by 4.1%, then decreased by 1.4%, while profits decreased by 135%, then increased by 71%. These movements don't seem to be correlated except that cost of goods sold increased by 2%, or $16,000, then decreased by 3%. If the cost of goods sold were held down in the second year, as expenses were, profits would not have taken such a dramatic drop.

Copy and use the blank forms to gather the data you need to analyze your own business.

RATIO COMPARISON BY MONTH

Business Name _____

Business Address _____

Ratios	Months						
Current Assets / Current Liabilities							
Sales / Working Capital							
Total Debt / Net Worth							
EBIT / Sales							
Net Profit / Net Sales							
Net Profit / Net Worth							
Net Profit / Total Assets							
Accounts Receivable × 365 / Sales							
Cost of Goods Sold / Average Inventory							
Fixed Assets / Net Worth							
Net Sales / Total Assets							

RATIO COMPARISON BY YEAR

Business Name _____

Business Address _____

Ratios	Years						
$\dfrac{\text{Current Assets}}{\text{Current Liabilities}}$							
$\dfrac{\text{Sales}}{\text{Working Capital}}$							
$\dfrac{\text{Total Debt}}{\text{Net Worth}}$							
$\dfrac{\text{EBIT}}{\text{Sales}}$							
$\dfrac{\text{Net Profit}}{\text{Net Sales}}$							
$\dfrac{\text{Net Profit}}{\text{Net Worth}}$							
$\dfrac{\text{Net Profit}}{\text{Total Assets}}$							
$\dfrac{\text{Accounts Receivable} \times 365}{\text{Sales}}$							
$\dfrac{\text{Cost of Goods Sold}}{\text{Average Inventory}}$							
$\dfrac{\text{Fixed Assets}}{\text{Net Worth}}$							
$\dfrac{\text{Net Sales}}{\text{Total Assets}}$							

EXPENSE COMPARISON BY MONTH

My Business: _____

Business Address: _____

Month							

Expense Item	Dollar Amount	%	Dollar Amount	%	Dollar Amount	%	Industry Average
Sales							
Cost of Goods Sold							
Gross Profit							
Expenses							
Drawings (Owner)							
Wages							
Delivery							
Bad Debt							
Telephone							
Depreciation							
Insurance							
Taxes (Local)							
Interest							
Advertising							
Miscellaneous							
Net Profit Before Taxes							

EXPENSE COMPARISON BY YEAR

My Business: _____

Business Address: _____

Year							
Expense Item	Dollar Amount	%	Dollar Amount	%	Dollar Amount	%	Industry Average
Sales							
Cost of Goods Sold							
Gross Profit							
Expenses							
Drawings (Owner)							
Wages							
Delivery							
Bad Debt							
Telephone							
Depreciation							
Insurance							
Taxes (Local)							
Interest							
Advertising							
Miscellaneous							
Net Profit Before Taxes							

Both the Pumping Iron Fitness Center and the Hi-Tech Merchandising Co. used debt to do most of their financing, as most new businesses do. The debt coverage ratio helps measure whether the firm can meet its payments or not—information that both business owners and creditors want to have.

Debt coverage ratios indicate a company's vulnerability to risk. The ratio shown below and the debt to net worth ratio provide the necessary tools to evaluate the safety of the firms.

TIMES INTEREST EARNED RATIO

Pumping Iron Fitness Center (third year)

$$\frac{\text{Earnings Before Interest and Taxes}}{\text{Interest}} = \frac{\$125,392}{\$22,447} = 5.6 \text{ times}$$

Hi-Tech Merchandise Company (third year)

$$\frac{\text{Earnings Before Interest and Taxes}}{\text{Interest}} = \frac{\$47,971}{\$11,500} = 4.2 \text{ times}$$

Measures: The extent that operating income can decline before the firm can't meet its annual interest charges.

Generally accepted standard: Depends on the industry, but six or seven times is a good target.

Low ratio means: A low margin of safety. The company may have difficulty borrowing.

High ratio means: It's good for the creditors. The company probably has borrowing capacity.

Remarks: Both firms are medium-low and should not consider adding more debt at the present time.

A variation of this ratio adds noncash charges such as depreciation, amortization and depletion to net earnings for cash flow coverage.

Pumping Iron Fitness Center (third year)

$$\frac{\text{Net Earnings} + \text{Depreciation}}{\text{Interest}} = \frac{\$98,385 + \$21,960}{\$22,447} = 5.4 \text{ times}$$

Hi-Tech Merchandise Company (third year)

$$\frac{\text{Net Earnings} + \text{Depreciation}}{\text{Interest}} = \frac{\$28,471 + \$24,000}{\$11,500} = 4.6 \text{ times}$$

Other fixed charges such as rent could be added to the interest payments to obtain a better idea of coverage.

Still another variation is called fixed charge coverage. This ratio recognizes that many companies lease assets and sometimes incur long-term obligations through the lease agreements. If your firm leases, this ratio may make more sense than the times interest earned ratio. It looks like this:

$$\text{Fixed Charge Coverage} = \frac{\text{EBIT} + \text{Lease Payments}}{\text{Interest Charges} + \text{Lease Payments}}$$

If these ratios are important to you, add them to the ratio comparison forms.

Your Turn

Do the following:

Use a blank piece of paper to calculate a ratio trend analysis and income statement analysis of the ABC Emporium.

Answers are in Appendix D.

LIMITATIONS OF RATIO USE

Ratios are more useful for small, focused companies and fairly autonomous divisions of very large corporations. Ratios don't tell much about a consolidated statement of very large international corporations.

Ratios are no substitute for insight, judgment and objective thinking. A company may change over time, making past ratios of doubtful value. Comparing companies of different ages is difficult, and seasonal factors, unexpected disasters or windfall profits greatly distort ratios and meaningful comparisons.

Ratios can also be skewed by companies using different accounting methods for expenses, earning money from investments rather than operations or planning for a low profitability now to build for the future. And leasing, renting, borrowing and payment practices can make ratios look good for this accounting period but not the next.

Ratios should always be compared to firms in the same industry. This can be done fairly easily, because several companies publish comparative ratio analyses.

Ratios are estimates, but they and industry averages are useful tools when properly applied with sound judgment and objective thinking. Nothing can consistently provide complete, detailed, accurate data. If there were, we wouldn't need good management.

CONTROLLING CREDIT

Controlling credit is one element of establishing a credit policy. Such factors as using a receivables aging schedule to keep outstanding credit in check, managing delinquent customers and collecting overdue bills are all ways to control credit.

ACCOUNTS RECEIVABLE AGING SCHEDULE

This technique can save you a lot of money and headaches. It's a simple tool. Just keep a record of those customers who have forgotten that they still owe you. A timely follow up, with an overdue notice to delinquent customers, can head off an account that may be lost forever.

The following table shows that the longer you wait to collect your accounts receivable, the less likely you are to receive full payment. This table assumes that you have the correct address and place of employment for a consumer or the address and a credit check for a business buying finished goods or raw material.

Past due by	Probability of collection
30 days	95%
60 days	82%
120 days	70%
6 months	49.5%

RECEIVABLES AGING SCHEDULE

HI-TECH MERCHANDISE COMPANY

END OF THE FIRST YEAR

ACCOUNTS RECEIVABLE AGING SCHEDULE					
			Past Due By		
Customer	Total	Current	30-59 Days	60-119 Days	120-180 Days
A	15,000	13,000	2,000		
B	12,000	11,000		1,000	
C	11,000	11,000			
D	14,000	11,000		3,000	
E	13,000	1,000	1,500	5,500	5,000
F	12,000	10,000	2,000		
G	3,000	2,000		1,000	
H	15,000	3,000	11,000	1,000	

Customer	Total	Current	Past Due By		
			30-59 Days	60-119 Days	120-180 Days
I	13,000	13,000			
J	2,000	2,000			
K	10,000	10,000			
L	13,000	2,000			11,000
M	17,000	15,000		2,000	
O	8,000	7,000	1,000		
P	6,000	3,000	3,000		
Q	16,000		500	4,500	11,000
R	3,000			1,000	2,000
Total	185,000	116,000	21,000	19,000	29,000
Percent	100%	62.7%	11.3%	10.3%	15.7%

Note: Days refers to calendar days, not working days

CREDIT COLLECTION TIPS

If you are unsure of the creditworthiness of a customer, run a credit check (your accountant can help you).

When checking potential credit customers, look for:

► Any hesitation in sharing financial information

► Any accounts receivable that are pledged to a loan institution

► Requests for purchases that are excessively large

► Other suppliers that have filed collection suits or obtained judgments

► Any frequent change of banks

No matter how careful you are, some customers will be slo
payers. When you experience financial problems:

► Restrict credit until past due bills have been paid

► Charge for carrying overdue accounts

► Accept a written promise from a senior officer

► Sell to past due accounts for cash only

► Work with customers to achieve a win-win situation (the customer must make sincere efforts to reduce back debt, pay something every month and make full disclosure of liabilities)

► Keep credit policies and procedures the same in good times as well as in bad times

► Begin early with overdue accounts; for example, call on the 31st day following shipment, and keep a record of the conversation

► Remind customers who promise to pay if you don't get a payment in 10 days

► Send a letter documenting your previous conversations with a stronger demand for payment after 40 days

► Have a lawyer call or write or use the small claims court after 50 days

► Use a collection agency after 60 days

► Stop actions after 90 days—you have probably lost all your profit and will lose more if you pursue it

Sometimes you may find it necessary to hire an outside agency for debt collection. When looking for a collection agency consider:

► Their reputation (were they recommended by others, have their past practices resulted in a high rate of collections)

► Their rates (an average commission is 20% – 25% of the amount collected; if it is higher, it may be too much; if it is much lower, say 10%, they may go after only easy claims).

▶ If the agency is bonded at least by $50,000

▶ If it maintains separate trust accounts or recommends that the debtor pay you directly

Get all the information well before you need it so that you won't be pressured into a deal that you really don't want.

THE IMPORTANCE OF WORKING CAPITAL

The need for quick access to cash is often forgotten in the entrepreneur's rush to start or expand the business. Money fuels the purchase of goods for resale or the equipment that will make money. But it is a mistake to think that continuing sales will finance all necessary new buys or pay off loans in a timely manner. Growth consumes money. Rapid growth consumes enormous amounts of money, and the money we are talking about is cash, not money to be paid later or money that will be available as soon as more goods are sold or customers come in.

A new business expects to grow. To control and manage this growth properly, cash must be available to support the sales. That's why we have liquidity ratios and insist that current assets be twice as large as current liabilities. The cash that supports sales is called working capital, which is current assets minus current liabilities. The ratio called the turnover of working capital is a function of sales. As sales increase, so must working capital.

As a general rule, goods are bought for resale or modification and resale. A business cycle develops: Order and stock inventory, pay for the inventory approximately 30 days later, receive the sales money still later and start the process again.

If credit is extended, the cycle lengthens for cash collection but stays the same for inventory reorder. Since you do not wait until all the goods are sold before reordering, you restock before you sell everything and collect for those sales.

The period between cash income and cash outgo is the time when working capital is critically needed. If business slumps because of the economy, a rainy day or increased competition, the delay to receive cash may be even longer. But suppliers want their money, and they can be very persuasive.

For our service business, goods are purchased for reuse. If the item is used quickly enough often enough and cash is collected before use, perhaps bills can be paid in a timely manner. But if use declines or is cyclic, you'll need cash during the lean times to pay the fixed expenses such as loans and salaries as well as variable costs.

Maintaining average working capital may not work if demand varies from month to month or quarter to quarter. For slow periods, a line of credit with your bank or lending institution is valuable. This should be in writing for the largest amount you can get. Establish your account long before you need the extra money, because when you need it to stay in business is when most lenders fear to give it out.

Working capital may be your biggest business worry, but it doesn't have to be if you stay on top of your needs.

REVIEW

► Trend analysis is an excellent technique to help you measure the direction of your business

► A month-by-month and year-by-year comparison will show your business trend

► Never run out of cash

► The accounts receivable aging schedule is a must if you do credit business

► The accounts receivable aging schedule will help remind you of those accounts that are past due and require special attention

► The credit collection tips will help you to avoid bad incidents with customers

► The debt coverage ratio information is useful for controlling your interest and fixed expenses and may be useful to your creditors

► Knowing and anticipating your working capital needs will help keep your business in balance and healthy

ASK YOURSELF

▶ Create your forms for doing a trend analysis.

▶ Describe your accounts receivable aging schedule.

▶ What are your procedures and policies to check credit applications?

▶ Discuss your plan and means to collect any overdue accounts.

CHAPTER
TWELVE

FINANCIAL
PLANNING

MANAGING YOUR MONEY

Small business owners make decisions every day. One of the most important decisions is how to use capital. To assess the benefits of an investment in new equipment or other expansion needs, it makes no difference whether the business earned the money or borrowed it. If you borrow the money, your lending institution will want to know how the money will be used and how it will be paid back.

To stay in business, proper financial planning is essential. The breakeven analysis and cost benefit analysis can help you decide if you should borrow money and how much, if you can pay it back promptly and if the project is worth a detailed evaluation, including discounted rates of return, a market analysis and detailed cash flow analysis. These decision-making tools can save you time and money. Use them.

BREAKEVEN ANALYSIS

The breakeven analysis is a good, cheap screening technique. It lets you distinguish between new product lines or service techniques and helps you make choices and determine if you should do a more intensive and costly analysis.

EXAMPLE

When you are deciding between a new product line or an increase in service, you must consider that both have cost implications. Costs obviously affect price and marketing feasibility. A breakeven analysis lets you compare the profits at different sales levels of different products.

The breakeven analysis lets you examine on paper your project's feasibility before putting up the money to try it. Breakeven analysis can be a substitute for estimating an unknown factor in making decisions. If most expenses are known, the other two variables, profit and demand, may vary. The breakeven analysis can help determine the cash flow, level of demand and combination of price and demand that will yield the anticipated profit.

Suppose one of the Pumping Iron Fitness Center owners has an idea for a new service and wants to get a quick feel for its feasibility and breakeven point. The following methods—charting and formula—show this.

The formula is: Breakeven sales = fixed costs + variable costs or

Be = F + V.

Two examples will show how this works.

Be = $100,000 + 66.6% Be

First we'll subtract 66 2/3% from both sides of the equation or = sign. (Remember on the left side the Be is considered one.) This results in 33.3% Be = $100,000. Now we'll bring the 33.3% back to the right side of the = sign. To do this, the rule is to place it under the $100,000, making it a fraction. Then divide 33.3 into the $100,000 for the answer or the breakeven point.

$$\frac{\$100,000}{.333} = \$300,000$$

The other breakeven point is one where the fixed costs have doubled to $200,000, and the variable costs are 55% of the breakeven point.

Be = $200,000 + 55% Be

Using the same method we have 45% = $200,000, therefore

$$\frac{\$200,000}{45} = \$444,000$$

The following charts illustrate the two breakeven points.

Drawbacks to Using Breakeven Analysis

A breakeven analysis lacks several important elements. It does not permit proper examination of cash flow. One good way to make investment or capital purchasing decisions is to consider the value of a proposed project's anticipated cash flow. If the discounted value of the cash flow exceeds the required investment cash outlay, then the project is acceptable, other things being equal.

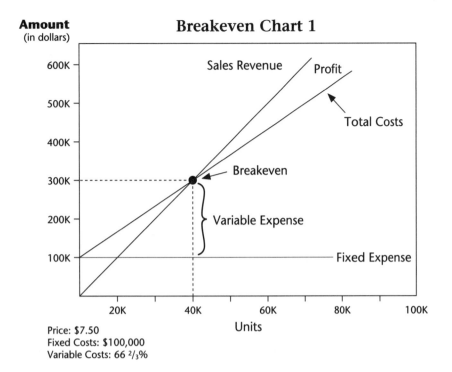

Amount (in dollars)

Breakeven Chart 1

Sales Revenue · Profit

Total Costs

Breakeven

Variable Expense

Fixed Expense

Units

Price: $7.50
Fixed Costs: $100,000
Variable Costs: 66 $^2/_3$%

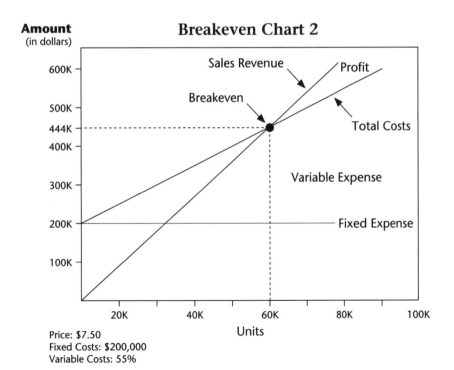

Amount (in dollars)

Breakeven Chart 2

Sales Revenue · Profit

Breakeven

Total Costs

Variable Expense

Fixed Expense

Units

Price: $7.50
Fixed Costs: $200,000
Variable Costs: 55%

The use of breakeven analysis requires that many restrictive assumptions about cost-revenue relationships be made. That is, a breakeven analysis is basically a negative technique, defining constraints rather than assessing benefits. Breakeven analysis is very static. It is good for a single point in time, not over a period of time.

Any business can find alternative uses for money. The breakeven analysis considers only one at a time and does not compare them. However, it is possible to compare two or more breakeven analyses.

The breakeven analysis is quite simplistic. It is a very good technique to determine if further study is feasible, but it should not be used for final decisions.

Working with borrowed money means risk, and risk under a period of high sales is heavily rewarded. But with low sales, borrowed money becomes a heavy burden to repay.

COST BENEFIT ANALYSIS

Cost benefit analysis means matching the available funds with the most beneficial use of those funds. This analysis provides a common basis for evaluating investment opportunities and projects for the company. Investment of scarce money also means that the benefit is for the long term, at least more than one year.

A cost benefit analysis works best if tangible items are compared; for example, two products or services or an old product or service with a replacement. The analysis measures the relationship between anticipated returns and costs and the anticipated return on investment.

	Old Product	New Product
Estimated sales items	100,000	125,000
Sales value @ $1.50/item	$150,000	$187,500
Cost of handling the items:		
$1.20 for the old item		
$1.25 for the new item	$120,000	$156,250
Gross profit	$30,000	$31,250
Benefit		$1,250

The annual benefit of $1,250 times the number of years the item proves to be of value to the business (assuming sales are constant) is the total benefit.

	Old Service	New Service
Estimated sales of memberships	200	250
Sales value @ $1,000	$200,000	$250,000
Cost of obtaining membership		
increase	0	25,000
Gross profit	$200,000	$225,000
Benefit	0	$25,000

The annual benefit is $25,000 per year if the membership rise equals the estimate and the membership does not fall. (These quick calcula-tion methods should be reduced by the expected inflation rate to get a discounted rate of return over the years of useful life or expected income, which can be done quickly with a business calculator.)

Reductions for inflation can be tempered with probability of success, taking the discounted income times a percent of success. The follow-ing table shows what happens if the new equipment has a useful life of five years and the income is discounted by 10%.

	Fairly Certain			Moderate			Risky		
Year	Income	Risk	New	Income	Risk	New	Income	Risk	New
1	$750	1.0	$750	$750	1.0	$750	$750	.9	$675
2	750	1.0	750	750	.9	675	750	.8	600
3	750	1.0	750	750	.8	600	750	.7	525
4	700	1.0	700	700	.7	525	700	.6	420
5	650	1.0	650	650	.6	420	650	.5	325
	$3,600		$3,600	$3,600		$2,970	$3,600		$2,545

If the cost of the new equipment, installation, disruption, training and other factors minus the salvage value is less than the risk, the product probably should be considered for investment or more study. The same technique can also be used to examine the rise in memberships.

	Fairly Certain			Moderate			Risky		
Year	Income	Risk	New	Income	Risk	New	Income	Risk	New
1	$25,000	1.0	$25,000	$25,000	1.0	$25,000	$25,000	.9	$22,500
2	25,000	1.0	25,000	25,000	.9	22,500	25,000	.8	20,000
3	20,000	1.0	20,000	20,000	.8	16,000	20,000	.7	14,000
4	15,000	1.0	15,000	15,000	.7	10,500	15,000	.6	9,000
5	10,000	1.0	10,000	10,000	.6	6,000	10,000	.5	5,000
	$95,000		$95,000	$95,000		$80,000	$95,000		$70,500

If the annual cost compared to the benefit modified by risk indicates that the new service is profitable, further study is warranted.

Your Turn

Answer True or False:

Cost benefit analysis does not allow you to use probabilities or the discounted rate of return.

The answer is in Appendix D.

Marginal Analysis

In marginal analysis, the income statement is revised to indicate whether the expenses are fixed or variable. This technique divides the amount of sales in two distinct parts. Part one is variable expenses (those that increase or decrease as sales increase or decrease), fixed expenses (which stay the same regardless of sales) and profits (which vary depending on sales and expenses). The second part is called the margin.

Answer True or False:

Marginal analysis will help you to understand how types of expenses can help or hurt you during both good and bad times.

The answer is in Appendix D.

The following example is based on the first year of the Pumping Iron Fitness Center. The second example is based on the Hi-Tech Merchandise Company's first year. Note the differences in the percent of variable and fixed costs for both firms.

Pumping Iron Fitness Center

Sales	200,000	250,000	300,000	350,000
Variable Costs (30%)	60,000	75,000	90,000	105,000
Margin Contribution (70%)	140,000	175,000	210,000	245,000
Fixed Cost minus Interest and Taxes	120,000	120,000	120,000	120,000
Operating Profit (EBIT)	20,000	55,000	90,000	125,000
Interest	25,000	25,000	25,000	25,000
Net Profit Before Tax	–5,000	30,000	65,000	100,000

Hi-Tech Merchandise Company

Sales	800,000	850,000	900,000	950,000
Variable Costs (80%)	640,000	680,000	720,000	760,000
Margin Contribution (20%)	160,000	170,000	180,000	190,000
Fixed Cost minus Interest and Taxes	128,000	136,000	144,000	152,000
Operating Profit (EBIT)	32,000	34,000	36,000	38,000
Interest	12,000	12,000	12,000	12,000
Net Profit Before Tax	20,000	22,000	24,000	26,000

The Pumping Iron Fitness Center had a gain of 42% ($150,000) in sales and reaped an 84% ($105,000) increase in operating profit—a gain of 50% profit. The Hi-Tech Merchandise Company had a gain of 16% ($150,000) in sales and reaped a 23% ($6,000) increase in operating profit—a gain of 30% profit on the same sales dollar increase as the Pumping Iron Fitness Center.

These figures show the difference between high fixed costs and low fixed costs. If the same percentages of sales gain were actually sales losses, the firm with the higher fixed cost would suffer more. Assessing risks on paper first can preclude a lot of sorrow later when real money is involved if the economy takes a dip. Do this for any business you might enter to estimate the risk and determine if it is worth it for you.

 **Your Turn**

Solve these problems to see if you understand how to do a breakeven analysis, cost benefit analysis, marginal analysis and probabilities. Answers are in Appendix D.

Breakeven analysis:

Be = Fixed cost + Variable cost

If fixed costs are $200,000 and variable costs are 75% of the breakeven point, what is the breakeven point?

Cost benefit

	Old Service	New Service
Estimated sales of memberships	500	600
Sales value @ $1,000	$____	$____
Cost of obtaining membership increase	0	55,000
Gross profit	$____	$____
Benefit	0	$

Probabilities:

This membership drive is expected to keep the new members for at least three years. Assume the new income is $45,000 per year. The income is discounted at 15% because of uncertainty.

Fairly Certain				Moderate				Risky			
Year	Income	Risk	New	Income	Risk	New	Income	Risk	New		
1	$45K	1.0	$45K	$45K	1.0	$45K	$45K	.85	$38.25K		
2	45K	1.0	45K	45K	___	___	45K	___	___		
3	45K	1.0	45K	45K	___	___	45K	___	___		
	$135K			$135K	$135K		___	$135K		___		

Marginal analysis

Sales	100,000	150,000	200,000	250,000
Variable Costs (25%)	25,000	_____	_____	_____
Margin Contribution (75%)	_____	_____	_____	_____
Fixed Cost minus Interest and Taxes	70,000	70,000	70,000	70,000
Operating Profit (EBIT)	5,000	_____	_____	_____
Interest	5,000	5,000	5,000	5,000
Net Profit Before Tax	_____	_____	_____	_____

ASK YOURSELF

▶ Explain breakeven analysis and how you can use it in your business.

▶ Discuss the differences between and advantages of breakeven analysis, cost benefit analysis and marginal analysis.

▶ What can be learned from fixed expenses and profit, variable expenses and sales?

▶ Describe the advantages of breakeven analysis.

CHAPTER THIRTEEN

EXPANDING YOUR BUSINESS

LEARN TO PLAN BUSINESS GROWTH

Expansion can come unexpectedly and quickly, or more slowly and properly planned. Business growth can come in many forms such as increased sales, increased profits, increased fixed assets, increased expenses, increased staffing, increased borrowing—increased everything except cash or money on hand. Unexpected and quick growth is not bad, if it can be handled. Expansion is expensive, so there is no use in making it so expensive that you can't afford it if you don't have to.

Overconfident management has been responsible for the demise of many an otherwise healthy venture. Many companies looked like they would go on forever, but they ended up on the scrap heap of forgotten dreams.

For some, understanding the value of planning for growth came too late. Business scrapheaps are littered with skeletons of one-person businesses that grew more than 2,000% in four to six years. The owners thought it would go on forever and fueled the growth with ever-increasing spending. Then one day the company stopped growing, and the cutbacks began. What was once a great place to work became an increasingly hostile environment.

Others were not so short-sighted. They slowed down their companies' growth while they absorbed the increasing volume of business. The process was difficult but, it gave them time to prepare themselves for more growth.

A comprehensive strategy is important not only to the start-up company but also to the mid-sized company. The question is no longer who I can sell to, since customers are now coming to you, but how I can have the latest technology to satisfy the increasing volume of business and my customers' needs and wants.

A management business strategy for expansion doesn't necessarily mean a plan for skyrocketing expansion. It does mean that the strategic planning should prepare for sustained expansion: to control that growth and to integrate it into a standard way of doing business. Fast growth is not a measure of business success if it doesn't include profitability or productivity.

Entrepreneurs and owners forget that obtaining more sales, receivables and inventory without increasing support from more people, equipment and storage invites disaster. These disasters usually come from owners' overconfidence and their desire to outstrip the competition.

Avoiding trouble is just one reason to plan growth. A more important reason includes the long-term strategic value of controlling growth, just as one controls other variables in the business equation. For instance: At any given time, no growth, slow growth or less growth may be just what is called for. Then you must be willing to forgo selling opportunities, limit your market share and keep money in the bank rather than spend it. Planned growth means that balance can be maintained, and that even rapid growth can be accommodated and does not have to ruin the company. Growth at any price can mean that the price is too high.

Let's say that now you want to expand your market. The three basic ways to do that are:

1. Market penetration, which means selling more of your current products to your established customers.

2. Market extension, which means enticing customers away from the competition.

3. New product or service introduction, which is persuading customers to buy something new.

MARKET EXPANSION

Market penetration may be a matter of training your sales people to ask the customer more questions about accessories, a larger model or more frequent visits. Increased involvement with customers may require more sales people. Increasing market penetration also may require more advertising, more or better services, in-store displays and public relations; longer hours and a larger parking lot or remodeling the store to make it more inviting.

Penetrating the market increases costs, which mount before expansion begins. Therefore a source of capital is needed and should be available before you begin.

Market extension is almost like starting a business. It is usually more costly, because you must identify and locate new custom-ers. You can do this market research yourself, but it takes time and money. After you learn who your potential customers are, you must determine how to reach and attract them. This calls for careful planning, detailed investigation and money.

New product or service introduction is probably the easiest method to increase sales, if the product or service is a good one. If the new product or service is not what old or new prospective customers want, then they may not want what they bought before. So a risk is involved as well as money.

OBTAINING COST INFORMATION

Control of the expansion is necessary, because each expansion method is expensive. To plan the growth, detailed cost information is required. Consider the following points when you seek cost information.

► Use all the information and experience you have developed.

► Your suppliers and vendors should be able to provide cost information and advice.

► Other business owners, as long as you do not compete directly, are usually happy to tell of their similar experiences. Those in your same business, but not in your trading area, are great sources. Find them through your suppliers, trade association or at trade shows.

► Your local chamber of commerce or federal or state Small Business Association office may have cost data.

When gathering cost data and information, get as much detail as possible, put it down on paper, refer to actual cost data, keep accurate records and note the difference between one-time and continuing expenses. When you begin to expand, frequently compare planned costs to actual expenditures and have a limit and contingency plan to stop, slow down or do something else if costs and the expansion begin to get out of hand. Planning is an absolute necessity, because changes made after you begin are the largest source of cost growth. You should always have a contingency fund.

Some rules of thumb from those who have gone through an expansion are:

- ► First guesses are always too low
- ► Best is the enemy of good—that is, start with what you think is good, because if you change it until you think it's perfect, you never will begin, and your money will have run out long ago
- ► The first 80% of the task takes 20% of the time and the last 20% of the task takes 80% of the time
- ► N + 1 trivial tasks take twice as long as N trivial tasks
- ► If anything can go wrong, it will

If hiring new people is part of your expansion, consider the time and cost to interview, process and train them. Use the table below to help you do this.

Function	Time	Cost
Job specification writing		
Job analysis		
Job description preparation		
Job announcement		
Application development		
Application review		
Interviewing		
Selection process		
Notification (selectees and nonselectees)		
Hiring procedures		
Training		
Follow-up		

Hiring takes time. Installing new equipment takes time. Designing new products takes time. These things take time, and your costs go on before even one dollar of extra or new business is generated. These are the costs you must be prepared for to stay successful.

Use this chart to see how long you can expect to wait before you see a return on your investment.

LONG-TERM ARRANGEMENTS

You will probably need some cash to help see you through your expansion. Most bankers will want to make short-term loans, but you may need longer terms. Here are a few reasons to help convince them to see it your way.

Amount of Time That Money Is Paid Out
Without Any Coming In

PREPARED BY: _____   DATE: __/__/__

TIME / EVENT		
1 Decision		
2 Order Equipment		
3 Hire Personnel		
4 Install Equipment		
5 Test Equipment		
6 Training		
7 OJT		
8 Full Production		
9 Shipping		
10 Receive Payments		
11		
12		
13		
14		
15		
16		

☐ Planned Task   ▨ Completed Task

Revision Date	Approval

△ = Single Event
☐ = Time Required
○—○ = Series of single events

Rapid growth in sales. A rise in sales usually means a rise in inventory, accounts payable and other expenses. It also means that revenue from those sales will lag behind the need to pay your expenses. If your growth is seasonal, short-term borrowing is appropriate. If the growth is expected to continue, a line of credit is in order. Carefully plan and chart the sales increase and expense outgo for the bank's information.

New market expansion. Increasing market share usually takes a long time. To secure a long-term loan, prepare spreadsheets with your bankers' help. Getting lenders involved early builds their confidence, makes them a part of your plan and makes it easier to get the loan arrangements you want. It takes time, but your chances of getting the money are much greater.

New product or service introduction. The loan you secure will depend on the time you project you will require to introduce the new product and estimated positive cash returns. It should be reasonable to expect repayments to match the anticipated positive change in cash flow. However, long-term loans are usually for mature companies with steady earnings. A rapidly growing company may need to consider leasing with an option to buy, rather than buying.

If you are asking for money for growth, be prepared for the following questions.

- ► What is your opportunity?
- ► How much will it cost?
- ► How much will success affect the balance sheet?
- ► How many resources are you committing?
- ► How much will your suppliers provide?
- ► How much money do you need from the bank?
- ► What are the risks and probabilities of failure?
- ► How or can these costs be absorbed if you must stop?
- ► When will you know to stop?

If you are having a problem with your present loan, be prepared for these questions.

- ► What is your problem?
- ► What caused it?
- ► What have you done so far to resolve it?
- ► How much money do you need from the bank?
- ► What will be the result of success?
- ► What will be the result of failure?
- ► Do you know when to quit?
- ► What alternatives do you have?
- ► How can you repay the loan if you fail?

Keeping your expansion on track requires that you plan and monitor your company's growth. Be sure you do all of the following.

1. *Set up a realistic cost system and keep it updated.*

   - ► Realistic costing must cover everything that goes into expansion
   - ► Remember the little things
   - ► Write it down and compare it to your plan

2. *Hold a regular review of expenses. Keep them adjusted to actual costs of doing business.*

   - ► Expenses should increase only as sales increase
   - ► Hold fixed costs steady, hold down production costs and monitor variable costs such as advertising and selling expenses
   - ► Check your budget to actuals at least monthly

3. *Review what the market is doing*

   - ► Spend time with sales
   - ► Maintain the contacts you made while building the business

4. *Obtain monthly financial analysis as soon as possible after the end of the month*

   ▶ The longer you wait to see what has happened, the harder it is to stop the bad trends and promote the good trends

   ▶ Treat your banker, lawyer and accountant on an equal footing with your other employees

5. *Hold weekly meetings with key personnel*

   ▶ Have a free flow of ideas. Discuss all problems.

   ▶ Don't skip a meeting just because you don't think there is anything to discuss—others may have something very important to say.

NEIL SMITH'S 14 RULES FOR EXPANSION

Neil Smith is president of NASCO Industries, the largest domestic producer of rainwear. Smith bought a nearly defunct rubber goods plant and turned it into a success. He began very small and expanded until it didn't make economic sense to increase production, hence sales. Listed below are his 14 rules for expansion.

1. *You must do the plan yourself*

   ▶ Know what goes into it

   ▶ Know where the data comes from

   ▶ Adjust it month to month and season to season

2. *Develop by segments*

   ▶ Sales and marketing

   ▶ Operations and financing

   ▶ Manufacturing and production

3. *Determine what the market will bear*

   ▶ Is there growth potential for this market?

   ▶ Who are your competitors and what are they doing?

   ▶ Where is the market and how do you get to it?

4. *Determine what your strategy is*

   ▶ Price

   ▶ Quality

   ▶ Service

   ▶ Policies

5. *Get your outside resources involved*

   ▶ Make your banker a "partner." Have clear communications.

   ▶ Your accountant and lawyer should be a part of your plan and assist in working with the bank

6. *Protect your current business*

   ▶ Know what would harm any existing business relationship you want to keep

   ▶ Be careful of buying advice

   ▶ Make and honor contracts

   ▶ Remember that lack of cash flow is the number one pitfall

7. *Run a very austere program*

   ▶ Remember that it will last from two to five years

   ▶ When buying equipment, you will receive no money until the equipment is paid for

   ▶ The employees won't earn you anything until they are trained

   ▶ Material payments are due in 30 days and labor is paid every two weeks, and

   ▶ Your money doesn't arrive for at least 90 days

   ▶ All equipment and functions of the business must carry their own weight

8. *When borrowing*

   ▶ Get as much as you can on a line of credit and get it in writing

   ▶ Always borrow long term for major equipment

9. *Money comes in from marketing, not manufacturing*

   ► New or unique items bring in more money

   ► It's more effective and efficient to get more from marketing than manufacturing automation

10. *It's easier and less expensive to modify an existing building than to build a new one*

    ► Buy

    ► Rent or

    ► Lease

11. *Control the growth*

    ► If price and quality are right, most customers may wait on their orders, but the goal is to service customers quickly

    ► Know your customers and the areas they serve

    ► Be available to your customers

12. *Know your business*

    ► Monitor receivables closely (weekly and even daily)

    ► Try to keep a proper proportion of payable and receivables

13. *During the first years*

    ► Don't expand into areas that aren't a part of your original plan

    ► Don't get sidetracked from your plan, and don't spend unplanned money

14. *People*

  ► Hire quality people, pay as best you can, work hard and cross-train

  ► Keep records and paperwork to a minimum

  ► Management never makes a product, your people do

  ► People are your quality control

  ► Key personnel are the sales manager, product manager, operations or office manager, buyer or purchasing agent, quality control, financial personnel, plant manager, industrial engineer, maintenance, production planner, personnel manager and supervisors. Many times these jobs can be combined and should be.

  ► Inform your employees of your plans, actions and proposed timetables

ASK YOURSELF

▶ List the sources of growth.

▶ Explain the difference between market penetration and market extension.

▶ Discuss the sources detailed cost information.

▶ Describe the biggest potential problem in expanding.

▶ Why should you set up a realistic cost system?

▶ What is the value of reviewing expenses once your cost system is operational?

▶ How can you benefit from maintaining outside contacts and monitoring the market after you put your plan into action?

▶ Why is it important to perform timely reviews of your financial statements?

CHAPTER
FOURTEEN

SELLING
YOUR
BUSINESS

PREPARE YOURSELF

A time may come when you want to retire or do something else and you decide to sell your business. There are three basic steps.

1. Prepare yourself

2. Value your business

3. Prepare your business to be sold

Preparing yourself is easy for some people but difficult for others. Usually those who are not prepared well in advance end up losing all or most of what they could have gotten if they realized someday they would have to step aside.

Your long range business plans should include ways to prepare yourself to eventually sell your business. This planning should start at least 5 years in advance of the date you plan to have your business sold. (Turnover within the family is a book in itself.)

One of the hardest things you may face is knowing that some-day you will have to let go of "your business." By preparing ahead of time may help you overcome any reluctance to selling your business as it becomes an ordinary part of doing business. However, giving up control over a business that you began and grew is difficult.

One of the worst events is not getting out of your business all that you put into it and this will happen if you wait until you or someone in your family is forced to sell your business in a hurry. So make your retirement a part of your business plan. To do this:

1. Get yourself in the right frame of mind by planning to sell your business as a normal course of events.

2. If you decide to taper-off by becoming a part of the selling package, of course do so but remember you will not be calling the shots for everything. Plan to work only part time on certain aspects and gradually decrease your time on the job. This should be part of the contract that also includes how much you are to be paid for your work.

3. If you do not have a hobby or other interests, develop one or more — you must have something to do besides worry about the business. There are lots of charities begging for

volunteers. You could use your time helping new entrepreneurs by giving advice on your own or through one of the organizations listed in Appendix A.

4. Prepare your family. Be sure to include them in your plan so that they know you will be under foot after a certain date. They should be included in your retirement plans.

5. Get your personal finances in order. Be sue of what you will have coming in from what ever sources will cover what you plan on doing. Check outstanding loans, continuing payments, and note any possible large purchases you may have to make. Also be sure your health and other insurance are in force and will continue as you want them to.

6. Finally make plans for right afterwards. If you are not going to continue working for a while, plan to get involved in something right away. This may be a lengthy trip, helping with your church or favorite charity or a civic association. Do something that signals that you have entered into a new part of your life—and have fun!

VALUE YOUR BUSINESS

Once you have decided that you are ready to sell, the next step is to determine the worth of your business or what you want to get for it. Most of the ways to put a value on a business involve very complex formulas and the use of a professional to develop them. But you can estimate a reasonable amount yourself by using a general purpose formula. One such method is four to six times the cash flow. (Cash flow is earnings before interest and taxes plus depreciation.) The more involved and complex your business is, the more time and help you will need to refine the asking price. However, the only real value of a business is the return it will bring on the new owner's investment. To calculate this, a method should use historical sales growth and earnings to project a future rate of return.

One popular formula is

$$\frac{\text{Income} \times (1 + \text{growth})}{\text{yearly rate of return} - \text{growth}}$$

In this formula, income is projected income, growth is the long-term rate of sales growth and the rate of return is what the buyer wants and is based on how risky the buyer perceives the investment to be.

To determine income, assess the last five or 10 year's income, subtract any income from other investments, expenses that are one-time-only payments such as insurance, a sale of part of the business or assets, any disasters that took unusual expenses or anything else that would distort a true profit picture, other things being equal. If you haven't been taking a fair salary for running your business, now is the time to get it right. If you have paid higher wages than normal to family members, now is the time to correct it. Do this for any extra-high rents paid or collected and any high business returns owing to weather or luck. Now average these incomes and reduce the average by the expected future tax rate. This equals income.

To determine your sales growth, measure your past growth and determine an average. Chances are that if you have been in business long enough, you should have averaged 4% to 8% in growth. If so, use that rate. If you can't determine your growth rate, use at least 4%. If you achieved more than 8%, know why and can prove it, use your figure. If not, use 8%.

Rate of return is the hardest figure to reach. If the business is risky, it must be high. The rate of return should be equal to or better than what "safe" investments will bring, plus the risk factor. This is often 14% to 32%. Remember, we needed at least 14% from our return on investment ratio to fund future growth. The risk factor could more than double this percent. We must select a percent that we believe our future buyer will insist on.

EXAMPLE

Suppose that the Hi-Tech Merchandise Company survived 15 years. Sales are projected at $2 million, the after-tax margin is 5% and the projected growth rate is 4%. We assume that the new owner wants at least a 20% rate of return.

$2,000,000 × .05 = 100,000 (income)

1 – .04 = .96 (1 + growth)

.20 – .04 = .16 (yearly rate of return – growth)

$$\frac{\$100,000 \times .96}{.16} = \$600,000$$

By using the four to six times cash flow method, let's assume that net profit became $80,000, interest lowered to $3,000, taxes stayed the same at $8,000 and depreciation was $15,000. $106,000 × 4 = $424,000; × 6 = $636,000. In this instance, both formulas are fairly close together.

Your Turn

Work the following problem using the future rate of growth formula to determine a value for the information shown below.

Projected sales: $5,000,000

Projected growth rate: 5%

After tax margin: 10%

Buyer's desired rate of return: 25%

The answer is in Appendix D.

Try evaluating your business or the Pumping Iron Fitness Center, assuming it lasted for 15 years or longer. Use the same projections, or make up your own.

You may want to have a valuation of your business for reasons other than selling it. For instance, you may want to purchase buyout insurance, if you are with a partner, or disaster insurance. You may want to plan your estate.

PREPARE YOUR BUSINESS FOR SALE

Now that you have determined what you might get for your business, it's time to convince others that your business is as strong as you think it is. The idea is to make the business attractive to an outsider.

Most buyers examine at least the last five years of financial statements. Thus, if you can, start preparing your statements with a sale in mind five years before you actually plan to sell.

To get the earnings in good shape, check for over compensation, perks, equipment or property rented to the business by the owner, entertainment expenses and any other items the business bought for the owners. Be able to explain any one-time costs, such as law suits, environmental or inventory problems and asset sales. Dispose of excess cash, investments and assets used for your purposes, such as boats and autos. This cleans up the financial statements to those figures that support only the business.

Document contractual relationships with vendors and suppliers, customers and key employees. Be sure any contracts are transferable to the new owner. Clear up any pending or in-progress law suits.

Organize your other documentation, such as your financial, business and customer plans and any other strategic plans that will be of value to the buyer. Assemble a plan that includes a list of factors that make your company attractive—anything that is unique—customer list, company size, types of jobs handled, special relationships with customers, a list of products or services, vendor list, market information, the real property that is to be sold, information concerning key employees, your availability to the new owner.

Look for potential buyers. The more you find, the better the bidding will be. Think about how the payment will be handled: all cash up front, a payment plan, stock swap or contract, and the conditions and terms of an agreement.

Sometimes it pays to hire an advisor, someone who is a professional at selling businesses. Hiring a person like this gives you more time to run your business, and you may need the extra help to keep your customers happy and restructure your financial statements to present the best picture possible. If you try to do too much now, it may adversely affect you later when you sell the business.

If you are considering using an agent, look for a company or person who:

► Has closed sales like yours

► Can locate buyers with an interest in your business

► You can get along with and trust

► Communicates with you regularly on your terms

► Sets reasonable fees based on what they will get for your business

Selling a business properly can take up to a year before all the details are resolved. Plan for many steps to take, meetings to attend and negotiations to settle, and don't be discouraged.

ASK YOURSELF

▶ What are the three basic steps in selling your business?

▶ Describe two ways to value your business.

▶ How many years should you go back to gather information about your business before planning to sell your business? Why?

▶ Discuss three things to do to get your business in good shape to sell it.

APPENDIXES

Appendix A
SOURCES OF HELP AND INFORMATION

Economic Development Administration
U.S. Department of Commerce
Washington, DC 20230
(202) 377-5081

Minority Business Development Agency
U.S. Department of Commerce
Washington, DC 20230

Small Business Administration
1441 L Street, NW
Washington, DC 20416
(202) 653-6385
(800) 433-7212

American Association of Minority Enterprise
Small Business Investment Companies
915 15th Street, NW
Washington, DC 20005
(202) 347-8600

National Small Business Association
1604 K Street, NW
Washington, DC 20006
(202) 296-7400

National Association of Small Business Investment Companies
1156 15th Street, NW
Washington DC 20005
(202) 833-8230

SCORE
The Service Corps of Retired Executives (SCORE) has more than 12,000 volunteer members in 592 offices around the country, to advise prospective business owners, regardless of age or status. Call (800) 368-5855 to find an office near you.

RATIO AND PERCENTAGE SOURCES
Dun and Bradstreet, Inc.
Public Relations Department
99 Church Street
New York, NY 10007

APPENDIX B
CAPITAL STOCK RATIOS

If you have or are thinking about going public with your business, you need to know about capital stock ratios.

The corporate financial statements are a little different from those for partnerships and single proprietors in that they include capital stock. The management of the corporation must report to its owners, the common shareholders, how the company performs. One of the reporting techniques used is capital stock ratios. Management must also exercise care in the handling of debt, and the use of ratios helps them do this.

This appendix will introduce four ratios that help an owner make decisions about the use of debt and equity. They are return on equity, earnings per share, price earnings ratio and the capitalization rate ratio.

In starting a business, all the money from the sale of stock would be shown under shareholders' equity as paid-in capital and under current assets as cash. If the corporation already existed, there would probably be some amount in retained earnings.

Without the use of stock to finance the corporation, there would be no need for capital stock ratios and the valuation of a share of stock for earnings or future growth. The value of a share of stock is the amount a buyer is willing to pay for it. For companies listed on a stock exchange, this is the market value.

Several factors make up this price. Those looking for income are interested in the dividends paid; those looking for future growth are interested in future earnings.

Common or capital stock ratios are used to determine return on equity. The price-earnings ratio is used to determine the amount potential investors want to have before investing. The capitalization rate is the reciprocal of the price-earnings ratio and measures the rate of return the market demands. Last, the earnings per share ratio measures the earnings each share of common stock has earned and is the amount available to each stockholder if management chooses to pay it all out. Our ratios and their analysis will be based on the following balance sheet and income statement.

JOG Corporation

Year End 19XX
Consolidated Statement

Current Assets	(000)	Current Liabilities	(000)
Cash	1,270	Notes Payable	500
Government Securities	407	Accounts Payable	408
Accounts Receivable	2,958	Accrued Expenses	449
Inventories:		Accrued Taxes	500
Finished Merchandise	3,300	Total Current Liabilities	1,857
Work-in-Process	775		
Raw Materials/			
Supplies	315	**Long-Term Debt**	
Goods-in-Transit	175	15 Year Notes	1,150
Total Inventories	4,565	10 Year Notes	1,000
Total Current Assets	9,200	Total Long-Term Debt	2,150

Property and Equipment		Shareholders' Equity	
Land	482	Capital Stock $1 Par Value	
Buildings	418	2,500,000 shares authorized	
Equipment	1,157	1,013,000 shares outstanding—Year 1	
	2,057	1,033,000 shares outstanding—Year 2	
Depreciation	903		
Total Fixed Assets	1,154	Paid in Capital	1,565

Other Assets		Retained Earnings	3,939
Prepaid Expenses	114	Total Shareholders' Equity	6,517
Foreign Receivables	56		
Total Other Assets	170		
Total Assets	10,524	Total Liability and Equity	10,524

JOG Corporation

Income Statement
Year End 19XX

Net Sales	$21,108,000
Cost of Goods Sold	13,546,000
Gross Profit	7,562,000
Operating Expenses	4,958,000
Operating Profit	2,604,000
Interest Charges	278,000
Earnings Before Taxes	2,326,000
Income Taxes (50%)	1,163,000
Net Earnings	1,163,000
Retained Earnings at the Beginning of the Year	3,080,000
	4,243,000
Dividends Paid ($.30)	304,000
Retained Earnings at the End of the Year	$3,939,000
Common Stock Shares Outstanding	1,013,000
Current Price per Share	$10.00

RETURN ON EQUITY RATIO (ROE)

$$\frac{\text{Earnings After Tax}}{\text{Shareholders' Equity}} = \frac{\$1,163,000}{\$6,517,000} = 17.8\%$$

Measures: The return on common equity or the return on the shareholders' investment. It measures management's ability to use effectively the owners' investment.

Generally accepted standard: Depends on the industry and what has happened during the business cycle (expansion, taking on debt, the economy). Usually the higher the better.

Low ration means: The owners or investors could have made more money investing in something else, if that was their aim. This should be examined against what else is or has happened.

High ratio means: Management has done well or they are hiding something until after the annual report. Usually the higher the better.

Remarks: This ratio is related to return on assets (ROA) when it is modified by an operating ratio and a leverage ratio. The ROE ratio will change because of variance in the turnover of operating assets, operating margin and financial leverage.

Return on Assets		Operating Ratio		Leverage Ratio	
$\dfrac{\text{EBIT}}{\text{Total Assets}}$	×	$\dfrac{\text{Net Profit}}{\text{EBIT}}$	×	$\dfrac{\text{Total Assets}}{\text{Shareholders' Equity}}$	
$\dfrac{\$2,604,000}{\$10,524,000}$	×	$\dfrac{\$1,163,000}{\$2,604,000}$	×	$\dfrac{\$10,524,000}{\$6,517,000}$	=
.25	×	.45	×	1.6	= 18%

EARNINGS PER SHARE OR BOOK VALUE RATIO

$$\frac{\text{Earnings After Tax}}{\text{Number of Common Shares Outstanding}} = \frac{\$1,163,000}{\$1,013,000} = \$1.15$$

Measures: Management's success in achieving profits for the owners. This is the amount available to the common shareholder after the payment of all charges and taxes for the accounting period.

Generally accepted standard: Depends on the industry and what the potential buyer or current shareholder is interested in (future growth or income).

Low ratio means: Management is not performing well when it comes to earnings.

High ratio means: The stock has a high rate of return on equity and will generally sell at higher multiples of book value than those with low returns.

Remarks: The usefulness of this ratio is questionable as little or no relationship exists between book value (based on historical costs) and market value, which is based on future earning and dividends. However, some analysts use this ratio in connection with another called market to book value ratio. It looks like this:

$$\frac{\text{Market Price Per Share}}{\text{Book Value Per Share}} = \frac{\$10.00}{\$6.43} = 1.5$$

The market value is 1.5 times higher than the book value.

This ratio tells if the market price is higher or lower than book value and by how many times, or, if it is lower, by what percent.

PRICE EARNINGS RATIO (P/E)

$$\frac{\text{Market Price Per Share}}{\text{Earnings Per Share}} = \frac{\$10.00}{\$1.15} = 8.7 \text{ times}$$

Measures: How much the investors are willing to pay per dollar of reported profits.

Generally accepted standards: Depends on the industry, what the individual investor wants to achieve and economic factors.

Low ratio means: The investors are not willing to pay very much for a share of stock. The potential shareholders consider the company to be risky. If the investor wants this stock and believes it will grow, the lower the ratio the better.

High ratio means: The investors believe that the company has a high growth potential, other things being equal. If the ratio is too high, investors may look for something more reasonable.

Remarks: This ratio and the others in this section indicate to management what the investors think about the corporation and its current, past and future performance. Generally, if all the ratios show good, steady performance, the stock will be high.

At the current earnings rate, an investor "gets" his money in 8.7 years, either in dividends or increased book value if not market value.

CAPITALIZATION RATE OR RATE OF RETURN RATIO

$$\frac{\text{Earnings Per Share}}{\text{Market Price Per Share}} = \frac{\$1.15}{\$10.00} = 11.5\%$$

Measures: The rate of return that the market demands for the corporation. As the P/E ratio increases, this ratio decreases.

Generally accepted standard: This ratio is the inverse of the P/E ratio and, like it, depends on the industry, what the investor wants and the corporation's objectives toward earnings.

Low ratio means: The investors consider the corporation to be a good buy because they don't demand a very high return on their money.

High ratio means: The investors want a high return for each dollar invested (it takes a large payoff to attract investors).

Remarks: Corporations that have high earnings growth generally have high prices in relation to earnings, and vice versa. The capitalization rate reports this in terms of a rate (percent) of return based on the selling price of a share of stock and the amount that the corporation earned on that share.

Appendix C
FRANCHISING

Franchising is a plan of distribution under which an individually owned business is operated as a part of a large chain. Services and products are standardized. The franchisor gives the individual dealer the right to market the franchisor's product or service by using the franchisor's trade name, trademarks, reputation and way of doing business. You usually have the exclusive right to sell or otherwise represent the franchisor in a specified area. In return, the franchisee agrees to pay either a sum of money, a fee, a percentage of the gross sales or both and sometimes buy equipment or supplies or some combination of the above.

Franchising covers about every business opportunity you can imagine. The prices range from very low to very high, you can work out of your home or a very elaborate facility, you can have little or no investment in buildings and equipment or a very heavy investment. It all depends on the type of franchise you select.

Advantages

▶ You need only limited experience

▶ Your financial and credit standing is usually strengthened when a national, well-known franchisor is behind you

▶ You obtain a well-developed image because the product is known, which helps your pulling power that may have taken years to obtain otherwise

▶ You acquire very well-designed and laid-out facilities, displays and fixtures

▶ You benefit from the chain's buying power

▶ National and regional promotion and marketing strategy is developed for you

Disadvantages

▶ You aren't the complete boss—you can't make all the rules

▶ You share your profits with the franchisor

▶ You are restricted in meeting local competition, adding or dropping products

▶ Some contracts may impose unreasonably high sales quotas, mandatory working hours or cancellation or termination of the franchise for minor infringements

- ► You spend lots of time preparing reports
- ► You may be a victim of any national franchisor's mismanagement or the company receiving a bad reputation

Under Federal Law You Have Several Rights

You have a right to receive a disclosure statement, usually at the first meeting with the representative of the franchisor. You have a right to receive documentation stating the basis and assumptions for any earnings claims that are made. You must receive these at least 10 days before you sign an agreement or pay any money.

You have a right to receive sample copies of the franchisor's standard agreement along with the disclosure statement. Final agreements must be given to you five business days before you sign them. You have a right to receive any refunds promised. You have a right not to be misled by oral or written representation.

Write for *The Franchise Opportunities Handbook*, which is available from the Government Printing Office, North Capital Street between "G" and "H" Streets NW, Washington, DC, 20401.

Franchise Checklist

- ☐ Has your lawyer reviewed the contract?
- ☐ Have you been asked to do anything that may be considered unwise or illegal?
- ☐ Do you have exclusive territory?
- ☐ Does the franchise company have any other business connections? Do you have any protection against a similar store opening near you?
- ☐ Do you know the termination terms?
- ☐ Do you know if you can sell the franchise to your advantage after building the business?
- ☐ Do you get assistance with training, public relations, credit, employee training, marketing and capital?
- ☐ Do you get help finding a good location?
- ☐ Do you know the financial condition of the franchisor? Is it adequate to provide assistance?

- [ ] Do you know the franchisor's staffing (experience and background)? Will they be there to help you?
- [ ] Do you have a reason to need this help?
- [ ] Have you been investigated carefully to assure that you can operate at a profit?
- [ ] Do you know your state's laws?
- [ ] Do you have the necessary money?
- [ ] Do you know your target breakeven point?
- [ ] Has a market study been done?
- [ ] Are you prepared to take the plunge?

Warning Indicators

▶ Unrealistic expectations about the amount of money you think you will make (half or more will be paid back to the franchising agency in one form or another)

▶ Unrealistic expectations about the amount of time you will need to spend in your business (60- to 80-hour work weeks 52 weeks a year are not uncommon)

▶ Idea that your money is not at risk (it is)

Remember that success will be determined by your tenacity—how hard you work.

Some new franchisors make unrealistic promises, so do some investigation before buying.

What to Look For

▶ A proven prototype location

▶ A strong management team

▶ Sufficient capital

▶ A recognized distinctive and protected trade identity

▶ Proprietary and proven methods of operation and management that have been included as an operations manual

- ▶ Comprehensive training program
- ▶ Field support staff
- ▶ Legal documents that reflect the company's business strategies and policies
- ▶ Market demand for the products and services

If You are Looking for a Particular Type of Franchise

Check for demographic trends and select the industry categories of franchises that fill those niches that are indicated by the trends.

- ▶ Check for growth forecasts in each franchised industry you are interested in
- ▶ Check the franchise association's membership applications for growth statistics for various types of franchises

When You Should Go Into Franchising

- ▶ If you need the experience and assistance of specialists
- ▶ If you can follow the franchisor's system
- ▶ If you will spend the necessary time and money to do a complete investigation of several franchisors
- ▶ If you can get the proper financing and you will spend the necessary time to research and seek the proper capitalization

You Should Not Go Into Franchising If

- ▶ You are knowledgeable about the field you want to enter
- ▶ You can generate more profits with a lower volume as an independent operator
- ▶ You must work just as hard and as long as if you were an independent operator

In the most successful franchise operations, both parties recognize that they need each other. The franchisee provides revenue, hard work and promotion. The franchisor provides systems, trademarks, support, advertising and the ability to negotiate volume discounts from suppliers.

Appendix D

ANSWERS TO YOUR TURN

Page 20

ABX STORE
Balance Sheet
Year End 19XX

ASSETS			LIABILITIES		
Cash	$2,000		Notes Payable	$18,000	
Accounts Receivable	85,000		Accounts Payable	205,000	
Inventory	210,000		Accruals	6,000	
Total Current Assets		297,000	Total Current Liabilities		229,000
Land/Building	50,000		Mortgage	25,000	
Equipment/Fixtures	50,000		Total Long-Term Debt		25, 000
Total Fixed Assets		100,000	Net Worth		143,000
Total CA and FA		$397,000	Total Liabilities and Net Worth		$397,000

STATEMENT

Net Sales (Less Allowance and Discounts)	$700,000
Cost of Goods Sold	500,000
Gross Profit	200,000

EXPENSES	
Drawings (Owner)	$ 74,000
Wages	65,000
Delivery	7,000
Bad Debt	4,000
Telephone	2,000
Depreciation	4,000
Insurance	7,000
Taxes (Local)	8,000
Interest	8,700
Advertising	3,000
Miscellaneous	2,000
TOTAL EXPENSES	$184,700

NET PROFIT (Before federal taxes)	$15,300

Page 24

Answers: 1. True 2. True 3. True

Page 36

► Start with more cash, increase cash received and decrease expenditures in the first month.

► No. An increase cash received or a reduction in cash paid out will, but starting with more cash will not. Remember cash flow only concerns cash in and cash out in the same month.

Page 43

$$\frac{\$41,000}{33,000} = 1.24 \text{ times} \qquad \frac{\$60,000}{6,000} = 10 \text{ times}$$

$$\frac{\$15,000}{23,500} = 64\% \qquad \frac{\$48,000}{23,000} = 2.09 \text{ times}$$

$$\frac{\$9,125,000}{60,000} = 152 \text{ times or days} \qquad \frac{\$25,000}{23,500} = 1.06 \text{ times}$$

If the top figure is accounts receivable and the bottom figure is net credit sales

$$\frac{\$2,000}{23,500} = 9\% \qquad \frac{\$60,000}{71,000} = 85\%$$

Page 49

CONSULTING R WE
BALANCE SHEET
2ND YEAR 19XX

ASSETS	DOLLARS	%	LIABILITIES	DOLLARS	%
Cash	15,000	25.3	Notes Payable	8,000	13.0
Receivables	10,000	17.0	Trade Payable	6,500	11.0
Inventory	2,000	3.4	Accruals	10,000	17.0
Investments	11,500	19.3	LTD Due	500	1.0

ASSETS	DOLLARS	%	LIABILITIES	DOLLARS	%
Current Assets	38,500	65.0	Current Liability	25,000	42.0
Fixed Assets	21,000	35.0	Long-Term Debt	14,500	24.0
			Net Worth	20,000	34.0
Total Assets	59,500	100	Total Liability	59,500	100

INCOME STATEMENT

SALES/RECEIPTS	$75,000	%/100

EXPENSES		
Drawings	$30,000	40.0
Wages	8,000	10.6
Advertising	3,000	4.0
Legal/Accounting	1,500	2.0
Maintenance	800	1.0
Supplies	250	.3
Telephone	1,800	2.4
Miscellaneous	150	.2
Depreciation	$3,000	4.0
Interest	1,000	1.4
Rent	10,000	13.3
Utilities	2,000	2.7
Insurance	750	1.0
Taxes/License	850	1.1

TOTAL EXPENSES	$63,100	84.0			%
			NET PROFIT	$11,900	16.0%

% = Percentage for Consulting R We   %IA = Percent of the industry average

Page 62

▶ *Are these ratios high or low compared to the standard?*

Standard is 2.2 times   High   Low   High   Low

$$\frac{\text{Current Assets}}{\text{Current Liabilities}} =$$ 1.7 ☐ ☑   2.6 ☑ ☐

▶ *Which would you want in your business?* The high one.

▶ *Why?* To be sure that there is enough cash to pay the bills.

Page 64

> ▶ *Are these ratios high or low compared to the standard?*

Standard is 9.6 times		High	Low		High	Low
$\dfrac{\text{Sales}}{\text{Working Capital}}$ =		10.7 ☑	☐	9.3	☐	☑

> ▶ *Which would you want in your business?* Neither.

> ▶ *Why?* The working capital is not adequate to support the sales. These ratios are not overly high, but they should be brought down by increasing current assets or lowering current liabilities or both.

Page 65

> ▶ *Are these ratios high or low compared to the standard?*

Standard is 60%		High	Low		High	Low
$\dfrac{\text{Total Debt}}{\text{Net Worth}}$ =		45% ☐	☑	65%	☑	☐

> ▶ *Which would you want in your business?* The low one.

> ▶ *Why?* This means that you have greater financial safety and can borrow if necessary.

Page 75

> ▶ *Interpret the following profitability ratio.*

The standard is 6.7%		High	Low
$\dfrac{\text{Earnings Before Interest and Taxes}}{\text{Net Sales}}$ =	3.4% ☑	☐

> ▶ *Would you want this ratio?* Yes.

> ▶ *Why?* It's better than a lower one, although it is not up to the standard. You should examine why, because there may be a logical, sound reason.

Page 76

▶ *Are these ratios high or low compared to the standard?*

Standard is 4.8% High Low High Low

$$\frac{\text{Net Profit}}{\text{Net Sales}} =$$ 5.6% ☑ ☐ 5.7% ☑ ☐

▶ *Would you want the first or second ratio or either?* Either, although the second one is one-tenth better.

▶ *Why?* Either one is higher than the standard, which means you are earning more than the average firm in your industry.

Page 78

▶ *Are these ratios high or low compared to the standard?*

Standard is 20% High Low High Low

$$\frac{\text{Net Profit}}{\text{Net Worth}} =$$ 12.7% ☐ ☑ 23.4% ☑ ☐

▶ *Which would you want?* The high one.

▶ *Why?* The return on your investment is better than the industry average. However, you should find out why. Is it efficient management, is the firm undercapitalized or are creditors a source of much of the capital? The last two reasons could be trouble.

Page 79

▶ *Are these ratios high or low compared to the standard?*

Standard is 5% High Low High Low

$$\frac{\text{Net Profit}}{\text{Total Assets}} =$$ 23% ☑ ☐ 7.8% ☑ ☐

▶ *Which is better?* The first one.

▶ *Why?* Although both beat the standard, the first one really beats it and indicates effective use of the firm's assets.

Page 89

► *Is this ratio high or low compared to the standard?*

Standard is 35 days   High   Low

$$\frac{\text{Accounts Receivable} \times 365 \text{ Days/Year}}{\text{Credit Sales}} = 35 \text{ Days} \quad \square \quad \square$$

► *Would you want this average collection period of time?* Yes.

► *Why?* It meets the standard.

Page 92

► *Is this ratio high or low compared to the standard?*

Standard is 5.5 times   High   Low   High   Low

$$\frac{\text{Cost of Goods Sold}}{\text{Average Inventory}} = 5 \text{ times} \quad \square \quad \boxed{\checkmark} \quad 7 \text{ times} \quad \boxed{\checkmark} \quad \square$$

► *Which would you want?* Either.

► *Why?* Both are near the standard and acceptable. If my average is too high, there is a danger of running out of stock sometimes; if it is too low, I am not moving much merchandise.

Page 93

► *Is this ratio high or low compared to the standard?*

Standard is 65%   High   Low   High   Low

$$\frac{\text{Fixed Assets}}{\text{Net worth}} = \quad 75\% \quad \boxed{\checkmark} \quad \square \quad 55\% \quad \square \quad \boxed{\checkmark}$$

► *Which is usually better?* 55%

► *Why?* More of your net worth is in liquid assets (such as cash and accounts receivable) than buildings and equipment. If trouble arises, you have more liquid assets to carry you—you may not be able to sell your fixed assets at a good price if you need the money.

Page 95

▶ *Is this ratio high or low compared to the standard?*

Standard is 4 times

$$\frac{\text{Net Sales}}{\text{Total Assets}} = 1.8 \text{ times}$$

	High	Low		High	Low
= 1.8 times	☐	☑	5 times	☑	☐

▶ *Which is usually better?* The high ratio.

▶ *Why?* You generate more sales with fewer assets than your competitors. The low ratio indicates that the assets are not pulling their weight.

Page 111

1. ▶ The current ratio is below the standard and needs to be increased by paying off more current debt or increasing sales.

2. ▶ The cash turnover ratio is only one-half the average and indicates a lack of working capital to pay current bills.

3. ▶ The debt to net worth ratio indicates that it is close to the standard and will probably be even closer next year as the mortgage and equipment are paid down.

4. ▶ The average collection period is 16 days longer than the average collection period. If this could be lowered, more money would be available to pay the bills.

5. ▶ The investment turnover ratio is only slightly below the standard, which probably indicates it is okay.

6. ▶ The rate of return on sales is higher than the average and shows that this firm could be very profitable if it can get control of its working capital and accounts receivable.

Page 122

1. Telephone, insurance, taxes (local), interest and advertising

2. Yes. The industry average is surpassed

3. $7,000

4. .9% = $6,300

5. The expenses are greater

Page 136

Total inventory cost = total carrying costs + total ordering costs

Total carrying costs = cost of money (.08) × average inventory value ($37,500) + storage costs ($3,000) + insurance costs ($100) + spoilage and theft costs ($100)

Average inventory value = Average inventory ($3,750) × unit price ($10) = $37,500

$$\text{Average inventory} \ = \ \frac{\text{Sales in units (150,000)}}{\text{No. of orders placed per year (20)}} \ =$$

7,500 divided by 2 = $3,750

Therefore the total carrying cost is $6,200

Total ordering cost = Cost to place an order ($20) + Cost to receive an order ($35) × Number of orders per year (20) = $1,100

The total inventory cost is $6,200 + $1,100 = $7,300

ABC Emporium

RATIO TREND COMPARISON

THREE YEARS

Ratio	1st Year	2nd Year	3rd Year	Industry Average
Current Assets / Current Liabilities	1.3 T	1.9 T	1.9 T	2.0 T
Sales / Working Capital	10.3 T	9.7 T	8.8 T	8.1 T
Total Debt / Net Worth	1.8 T	1.5 T	1.2 T	.80%
EBIT / Net Sales	3.4%	3.9%	4.0%	4.8%
Net Profit / Net Sales	2.2%	2.4%	2.6%	3.2%
Net Profit / Net Worth	10.7%	14.7%	11.0%	16.0%
Net Profit / Total Assets	3.8%	4.0%	4.2%	8.9%
Accounts Receivable × 365 / Sales	44 D	37.7 D	46 D	33.0 D
Cost of Goods Sold / Average Inventory	2.4 T	3.7 T	3.4 T	5.5 T
Fixed Assets / Net Worth	70%	68.2%	64%	50%
Net Sales / Total Assets	1.8 T	1.6%	1.6%	2.9 T

T = Times; D = Average number of days it takes to collect credit sales

ABC Emporium

INCOME STATEMENT ANALYSIS

THREE YEAR COMPARISON

Expense Item	1st Year		2nd Year		3rd Year		Industry Average
	Dollar Amount	%	Dollar Amount	%	Dollar Amount	%	%
Sales	700,000	100	725,000	100	750,000	100	100
Cost of Goods Sold	500,000	71	522,000	72	540,000	72	71
Gross Profit	200,000	29	203,000	28	210,000	28	29
% Increase in Sales (annual)		3.4		3.3			
Drawings (owner)	74,000	10.6	74,000	10.2	74,000	9.9	8.4
Wages	65,000	9.3	65,000	9.0	75,000	10.0	10.4
Delivery	7,000	1.0	11,000	1.5	9,000	1.2	1.4
Bad Debt	4,000	.6	4,000	.6	4,000	.5	.7
Telephone	2,000	.3	2,000	.3	2,600	.3	.4
Depreciation	4,000	.6	4,000	.6	4,000	.5	.5
Insurance	7,000	1.0	7,300	1.0	7,500	1.0	.7
Taxes (local)	8,000	1.1	8,000	1.1	8,000	1.1	.3
Interest	8,700	1.2	8,700	1.2	8,700	1.2	.6
Advertising	3,000	.4	4,000	.6	5,200	.7	.8
Miscellaneous	2,000	.3	2,500	.3	4,000	.5	.8
	$184,700	26.4	$190,500	26.4	$202,000	26.9	25.0
Net Profit	15,300	2.2	12,500	1.7	8,000	1.1	3.0

Page 163

ABC Emporium ratio trend analysis

The current asset to liabilities ratio is moving in the right direction and the sales to working capital ratio is coming down. The total debt to net worth is above the industry average of 80%; however, it is heading in the right direction. The earnings before interest and taxes are slowly moving up and, as sales increase or expenses are held down, it should come close to the industry average. The profit to sales is also below average but should improve as interest payments decline, sales increase and expenses are contained.

The return on investment rose, then fell and is short of the average. This should increase as business increases and expenses are held down.

Net profit to total assets is rising, but not too fast, and is still not close to the average. Right now there are too many assets to support the sales, but this business is only three years old. This ratio should improve.

Collection of credit sales was moving in the right direction, then slipped. Perhaps the owner extended the credit terms to increase sales. If so, collection efforts should increase before more time elapses.

The inventory turnover dropped a little, which probably means that the company is still overstocked. The cash position hasn't changed too much.

Fixed assets as a part of net worth is staying below 75% and dropping to an average of 50%, which may be due in part to the increase in working capital. The turnover of sales to total assets is not moving toward the averages, perhaps because of too much inventory or insufficient sales for the amount of assets. This ratio should be calculated using fixed assets to see if they are in line. So there is good news and bad news for the ABC Emporium, but, overall, progress is being made.

ABC Emporium expense analysis

The cost of goods sold is staying within 1% of the average, but 1% is $7,500. That's a lot of money to lose. The first element of good expense control is to buy smart, which puts extra money in your pocket before you sell anything. Sales have increased each year, but the second year was at a decreasing rate. This deceleration needs to be investigated because, as shown by the ratio trend analysis, the company's assets should support more sales or be reduced. Perhaps the owner is not taking advantage of trade discounts or paying premium prices when competitors are not.

The owner's drawings are a little high, which may not mean anything if the owner is using part of that money to help the business (such as by paying bills and thus helping working capital) and it doesn't appear on this statement. However, the trend is in the right direction. The employee wages are a little low but rising as sales increase, and the low percent could be owing to the business location.

Bad debt and telephone expenses are below average, which helps net profit and may also be owing to the location of the business. Delivery expenses have varied and now appear to be on track, but insurance expenses are higher than average. The owner should investigate what items are included in these industry averages, because, for example, items of delivery expense such as gas and vehicle insurance may be located in other categories, which will skew the figures. Only the comparison of like items will give a true picture of the business. Perhaps the owner can just get a cheaper deal on insurance.

Depreciation is on target but may fall below the average unless more or newer equipment is added or the building is expanded or revamped.

Taxes are very high, and this situation should be investigated. Special assessments, a desirable location, a political situation or an honest bureaucratic mistake can result in a high tax bill, but this expense needs attention. Interest is also too high, but this expense may be justified because a new business will carry a higher debt. The owner should check that the businesses in the industry average are the same age as the ABC Emporium. If so, apparently most like businesses used more equity capital to finance their start-up.

The advertising budget is rising with sales and is below average. Advertising could be increased to attract more business. Miscellaneous expenses are moving with sales and are below the average, which is good if we are comparing like sales and like items in the miscellaneous category.

Net profit is lower and falling even lower despite rising sales. At least 1% of this is in the cost of goods sold and another 1.5% is the owner's salary. If these numbers were corrected, this business would be ahead of the average net profit. Radical changes, such as buying cheaper goods, should be avoided, because such changes adversely affect your business if your customers expect high-quality merchandise.

Page 178

Answer: False. Cost benefit analysis can use probabilities.

Page 179

Answer: True. It offers you a look at what might happen under sales increases or decreases.

Page 180

Breakeven analysis:

Be = Fixed cost + Variable costs

Fixed cost = $200,000

Variable costs = 75% Be

Be = $200,000 + 75% Be

$.25 \text{ Be} = \$200,000 = \dfrac{\$200,000}{.25} = \$800,000$

$800,000 Be = $200,000 Fc + $600,000 Vc

Cost benefit

	Old Service	New Service
Estimated sales of memberships	500	600
Sales value @ $1,000	$500,000	$600,000
Cost of obtaining membership increase	0	55,000
Gross profit	$500,000	$545,000
Benefit	0	$ 45,000

	Fairly Certain			Moderate			Risky		
Year	Income	Risk	New	Income	Risk	New	Income	Risk	New
1	$45K	1.0	$45K	$45K	1.00	$45K	$45K	.85	$38.25K
2	45K	1.0	45K	45K	.85	38.25K	45K	.70	31.50K
3	45K	1.0	45K	45K	.70	31.50K	45K	.55	24.75K
	$135K		$135K	$135K		114.75K	$135K		$94.50K

Marginal analysis

Sales	100,000	150,000	200,000	250,000
Variable Costs (25%)	25,000	37,500	50,000	62,500
Margin Contribution (75%)	75,000	112,500	150,000	187,500
Fixed Cost minus Interest and Taxes	70,000	70,000	70,000	70,000
Operating Profit (EBIT)	5,000	42,500	80,000	117,500
Interest	5,000	5,000	5,000	5,000
Net Profit Before Tax	0	37,500	75,000	112,500

Page 202

$$\frac{\text{Income} \times (1 \ \text{growth})}{\text{Yearly rate of return growth}}$$

$\$5,000,000 \times .10 = 500,000$ income

$1 - .05 = .95$ growth

$.25 - .05 = .20$ yearly rate of return – growth

$\$500,000 \times .95 = \$475,000$

$$\frac{\$475,000}{.20} = \$2,375,000$$

ABOUT THE AUTHOR

James O. Gill, M.S., has been actively engaged in engineering and analytical management for over twenty years. He was a Division Manager and a Projects Manager with the Naval Weapons Support Center in Crane, Indiana. Gill presents papers at both national and international conferences and provides leadership at business seminars. He is the author of the best-selling *Understanding Financial Statements* and *Financial Analysis,* also published by Crisp Publications, Inc.

Gill is founder of JOG and Associates, a consulting firm in Indiana.

NOTES

NOTES

THE U.S. CHAMBER OF COMMERCE
SMALL BUSINESS INSTITUTE

We hope that you found this book beneficial to the success of your operation. For additional materials from the Small Business Institute, refer to the listing below. A free catalog is available upon request from the Small Business Institute, 1200 Hamilton Court, Menlo Park, California 94025. Phone: 800-884-2880

While you are learning, you can also earn a Small Business Institute Certificate of Completion along with valuable continuing education units (CEUs).

Course materials:	Order Numbers:
Marketing and Sales	
Marketing Strategies for Small Businesses	172-4
Prospecting: The Key to Sales Success	271-2
Direct Mail Magic	075-2
Professional Selling	42-4
Writing and Implementing a Marketing Plan	083-3
Budget and Finance	
Financial Basics of Small Business Success	167-8
Budgeting for a Small Business	171-6
Extending Credit and Collecting Cash	168-6
Getting a Business Loan	164-3
Personal Financial Fitness	205-4
Legal Issues	
A Legal Guide for Small Business	266-6
A Manager's Guide to OSHA	180-5
Rightful Termination: Avoiding Litigation	248-8
Sexual Harassment: What You Need to Know	312-3
The A.D.A.: Hiring, Accommodating and Supervising Employees with Disabilities	311-5
Human Relations and Communications	
Human Relations in Small Business	185-6
Attacking Absenteeism	42-6
Quality Interviewing	262-3

Effective Performance Appraisals   196-1
Working Together: Succeeding in a   292-5
  Multicultural Organization

Improving Productivity
Avoiding Mistakes in Your Small Business   173-2
Personal Time Management   264-X
Organizing Your Workspace   125-2
Attitude   317-4
Better Business Writing   25-4

Quality and Customer Service
Great Customer Service for Your Small Business   364-6
Telephone Skills from A to Z   301-8
Calming Upset Customers   65-3
Measuring Customer Satisfaction   178-3
Quality Customer Service   203-8

Supervision, Management, and Leadership
Building Teams for Your Small Business   365-4
Rate Your Skills as a Manager   101-5
Managing Negative People   306-9
Project Management   75-0
Giving and Receiving Criticism   23-X

U.S. CHAMBER OF COMMERCE

SMALL BUSINESS INSTITUTE™

The publisher of books for the U.S. Chamber of Commerce Small Business Institute is Crisp Publications. Crisp offers over 200 other business and entrepreneurship titles. For more information, call the U.S. Chamber of Commerce Small Business Institute at 800-884-2880.

CRISP PUBLICATIONS